LIVE YOUR

BEST LIFE

WITH LIMITED ENERGY

Successfully Manage ME/CFS,

Long COVID, and Other

Chronic Fatigue Conditions

Jodie Renner, M.A.

Live Your Best Life with Limited Energy –
Successfully Manage ME/CFS, Long COVID,
and Other Chronic Fatigue Conditions

Author: Jodie Renner

ISBN: 978-1-7390230-0-3

Published by Cobalt Books, Kelowna, B.C., Canada

Cover Design by Custom Designs by Jenn

Most of the photos are by Jodie Renner

Note: Thirty percent (30%) of the proceeds from the sale of this book will go to the Bateman Horne Center, a highly respected non-profit organization that helps people with ME/CFS through clinical care, research, and education.

Important: This book is in no way intended to offer medical advice. Please consult a trusted health professional for medical diagnoses and guidance.

Your Feedback is Welcome and Encouraged

This book was written entirely by someone with ME/CFS (myalgic encephalomyelitis/chronic fatigue syndrome) and the accompanying fatigue, intermittent brain fog, and other symptoms.

Feedback:

If you have an energy-limiting chronic condition of any kind (or are a caregiver), I welcome your opinion on anything you might consider inaccurate and/or suggestions about anything you think should be included in this book. Please email me at info@jodierenner.ca. If I agree with your suggestions, I will be happy to make the changes.

Reviews:

If you find this book helpful and think others would benefit from it, please **write a review** on the Amazon site where you purchased it and/or on Goodreads.

Share with others:

Also, to reach more people who are struggling with energy deficits and help them benefit from the suggestions and tips in this book, please tell others about it on social media groups for people with ME/CFS or long COVID.

Help others:

30% of the profits from the sales of this book will go to the Bateman Horne Center, a highly respected non-profit organization that helps people with ME/CFS through clinical care, research, and education.

Thank you.

Jodie Renner, author

Dedicated to the millions of people worldwide, most of them undiagnosed, who have unexplained debilitating fatigue and struggle every day to manage even minor tasks.

Some of the Reviews of
Live Your Best Life with Limited Energy

Handbook for life

"I have M.E. and have bought a lot of books, attended a lot of help groups, and never really had things put as simply and helpfully as this, all in one place. […]

"It's like having a big sister reminding you to be kind to yourself, to put you first, and all the simple things to save energy that are straightforward but somehow become lost in amongst the life of living with pain and illness.

"Wish I'd have had it 23 years ago, but happy to have it now."

- Stephanie, UK

So helpful

"I found this book insightful and personal. It's about not only how to live with ME/CFS, but with any illness or medical condition that leaves you exhausted and struggling to cope each day.

[…] the author takes you by the hand and speaks to you as if she was beside you as she gives you helpful hints and advice. It's obvious she's been there and understands 100% what it's like.

"This book is filled with lots of great ideas for maintaining energy while truly living your best life."

- S. Tucker, Canada

A Valuable Guide

"This book can help anybody dealing with chronic pain or fatigue. Jodie Renner gives us permission to feel our pain and slow down when we need to. As someone who has felt pressure to push myself, it's so helpful to hear what Ms. Renner has to say about the "crashes" that happen when we do too much. .... A helpful and friendly guidebook for the chronically ill and their loved ones."

- Anne R. Allen, US

Very comprehensive, helpful, and easy to read

"This book is very affirming and is jam-packed with helpful ideas to make life easier and better for people with chronic or long-term fatigue problems, regardless of the cause. It shows how to conserve limited energy so it can be used for the most important things in the person's life."

- Laurie, Canada

A must-read for anyone dealing with chronic low energy!

"Five stars for this book which covers all sorts of tricks and tips for getting the most out of limited energy supply. [...] If you have arthritis, chronic fatigue, fibromyalgia or long Covid, or any other illness that makes you tired then it will be helpful to you.

"I especially liked how it was broken into little paragraphs as that was much easier to read and to remember.

"Jodie Renner writes clearly and succinctly, and her knowledge of this subject is obvious. Highly recommend."

- Michele Rule, Canada

Table of Contents

ADDITIONAL INFORMATION ON ME/CFS & OTHER CONDITIONS

Introduction

How This Book Can Help You

These tips are aimed to help anyone with chronic fatigue and other energy-limiting issues.

This practical, to-the-point, easy-to-read handbook will help anyone with ME/CFS (myalgic encephalomyelitis/chronic fatigue syndrome), long COVID, fibromyalgia, Lyme disease, Ehlers-Danlos syndrome, lupus, MS, arthritis, ageing, or any other condition that causes fatigue, muscle weakness, brain fog, and mobility issues (among other symptoms).

You'll find:

Day-to-day advice and hacks to save your limited energy in hundreds of small ways, so you can free up energy for activities you enjoy and would like to do more.

Strategies for increasing your overall energy level and sustaining it at a more productive level.

Tips for seniors too, and those convalescing. These reader-friendly strategies will also be a great help to older seniors with fatigue, muscle weakness, cognitive and mobility issues, and anyone recovering from surgery or a serious illness.

Help with independent living. The tips are especially useful for those living alone and looking for ways to stay self-sufficient and independent for as long as possible.

A reader-friendly format. This book is designed to be easy to read for someone with difficulty focusing on the printed page. It's in a larger font (typeface), with lots of white space, short paragraphs, bolded headings and subheadings, and bulleted lists to make the information easy to find.

Easy navigation. In the e-book version, just click on the heading or subheading in the Table of Contents, and you'll jump to that spot in the book. Then click on "Back to Table of Contents" to instantly return to the list of topics.

Personal experience over decades. I developed and gleaned these tips from over fifty years of living with ME/CFS and from courses I've taken through the Complex Chronic Diseases Program in Vancouver, BC, Canada, as well as a great deal of online research. I also include some anecdotal advice from people I know personally and others on various social media groups for those with myalgic encephalomyelitis, long COVID, and fibromyalgia.

Some advice from the experts. I've done some of the basic research for you by locating expert advice on the web and condensing and paraphrasing the most relevant, essential, and useful info here.

You won't find:

Miracle cures or medical advice in this book—just practical tips, useful strategies, and helpful aids for conserving and increasing your energy so you can live a more satisfying life. I learned over time how to navigate this challenge, and I hope the advice here will make your journey easier.

How to Approach this Book

Read in any order. Go directly to topics that interest you.

Feel free to jump around and read the chapters in any order. There's no need to start at the beginning and read to the end. That would be too tiring and might discourage you from continuing.

Just read the Table of Contents, then go to any topics that interest you now, and come back later to read other topics.

In the e-book, just **click on a chapter in the Table of Contents to jump to that chapter**, then click in "Return to Table of Contents" to go back.

Critical information appears more than once.

Those of you who read this entire book will find some repetition of essential information. I hope you'll excuse that. Many or most readers will jump around and only read chapters that interest them. I would hate to see some readers miss out on critical information because they were too fatigued to read every chapter.

Important: This book is in no way intended to offer medical advice. Please consult a trusted health professional for medical diagnoses and guidance.

NAVIGATING YOUR (NEW) REALITY

You Found Your People!

"I'm not the only one! There are others like me!"

That's how I felt when, after more than fifty years of struggling with chronic fatigue, I was finally officially diagnosed with myalgic encephalomyelitis (ME/CFS), was accepted into the Complex Chronic Diseases Program (CCDP), out of the Women's Hospital in Vancouver, BC, Canada, and started participating in their year-long, very helpful Zoom classes.

That feeling of finally being validated and the sense of belonging were further enhanced when I joined about seven Facebook groups (more than double that now) for people with ME/CFS, fibromyalgia, or long COVID.

I found out there were many others with limited energy, brain fog, and muscle weakness out there. I no longer felt like a wimp, a drag, a party-pooper, an outsider.

On top of the fatigue and lack of endurance, I was (and am) also sensitive to cold, heat, bright lights, loud noises, and strong scents, as well as certain foods. Turns out that almost everyone with ME/CFS is sensitive to these conditions, especially when we're fatigued or in a crash.

All those pre-diagnosis years, I also felt I had to push myself physically to keep up with others on walks or hikes, despite knowing I would be useless the next day—or for several days or a week. I'd never heard of PEM (post-exertional malaise) or "crashing" after overdoing it. I only knew that it happened to me. I also didn't realize that a crash can be delayed by up to 72 hours, so the next day you might feel okay, then a day or two later, it's like you've been hit by a ton of bricks!

I always loved dancing but could only go to one lesson a week (I only lasted about 40 minutes of the 55-minute class) and one dance a week (and I had to leave after an hour or so because I was too exhausted to continue). I would try to sneak out quietly, but friends I sat with or danced with would often say, "What? You're leaving already? The night has just begun!"

So I would make up excuses, like "My (foot/ankle/knee/back) is bothering me," or "I have to get up early tomorrow morning," or "I'm (going away/having company) tomorrow, and I have to finish getting ready," or whatever would make me seem more "normal" in their eyes.

Have you felt you had to *fake being well* to fit in with your peers?

Probably everyone with an energy-limiting condition has. We want to belong, not stand out or be pitied.

A year and a half ago, in March 2022, my condition was still mild, and I was excited about finally going away on a trip, after being cooped up for two years during the pandemic. The excitement and adrenaline fooled me into thinking I had way more energy than I really had, so I seriously overexerted on the 5-day vacation.

Climbing big hills and many floors of stairs, rushing around, not enough rest, and no naps caused my condition to go from mild (functioning out in the world with modifications) to moderate (mostly housebound, with low energy, muscle weakness, and brain fog).

On my return, I crashed for a week, but didn't recover to my former baseline. After a few months, I realized I had to give up my successful book editing career and shut down my editor-author website. Now, I can no longer dance or hike or enjoy a lively gathering of several people at a noisy venue.

I've learned to accept my current situation and, by staying tuned in to my body and making smarter decisions each day, use what extra energy I generate to create a meaningful, satisfying life.

We may not be able to hike up mountains, play fast sports, or go on adventure trips like some of our friends can, but if we stay positive, respect our bodies, and avoid pushing ourselves, we can learn ways to manage our condition and enjoy life more.

> A secret to happiness is letting every situation be what it is instead of what you think it should be, and then making the best of it.
>
> @_yungbleu / Twitter

How We Differ from Our Healthy, Fit Friends

Whether you have ME/CFS, long COVID, fibromyalgia, or another energy-limiting condition, your physical and cognitive abilities are now different from those of healthy, fit people you know.

Some of the ways our reactions are different from others who are healthy and fit:

Normal activities tire us out much more.

Some people I know can hike or take a long bike ride during the day, then go to a dance, concert, or other event that same evening. That amazes me. Many of us with chronic fatigue can only do one "extra" thing—like going to lunch with a friend or grocery shopping—every two or three days, with rest days in between. Some of us rarely make it out of the house. Others are bedbound.

Brain fog hinders our focus, concentration, and memory.

Often, or when we're in a crash, we can find it difficult to converse, read, write, work on puzzles or hobbies, or watch a movie or TV show.

Remaining upright for lengthy periods is often difficult.

Many of us suffer from orthostatic intolerance, especially when overtired. Some of us may have POTS, which makes it difficult for us to stand up or walk for long. See the chapters on those.

Social interactions are often draining.

Trying to follow and participate in a conversation is really demanding on our fatigued brains, and that's multiplied when we're attempting to converse with more than one person.

Phone calls can be exhausting, and even texting back and forth can be tiring.

We're more sensitive to heat and cold.

To prevent exhaustion, we need to avoid temperature extremes and dress accordingly when going out. Be sure to stay out of the sun on a hot day.

We're sensitive to bright light.

When I'm tired, it's like the bright sun is searing through my eyeballs and into my brain. Sunglasses and a hat with a brim give me relief.

Loud noises and music are exhausting.

They make us stressed, increase our fatigue, can give us a pounding headache, and make us want and need to retreat to a quiet place.

Strong scents can give us a headache and nausea.

The smell of perfumes, colognes, diesel fumes, rubber tires, and other chemical smells make many of us feel ill, including headache and nausea.

Stress can exhaust us for days, weeks, or longer.

To conserve our energy, it's extremely important to find ways to stay as calm as possible. You'll find ideas for this in several places in this book.

Overexertion will set us back way too much.

Pushing ourselves when we're tired can even cause permanent damage. It could take us days, weeks, months, or even years to recover after severe exertion. Pay constant attention to your body when exercising and stop before you're overtired. Then wait a few days to see if what you did caused a crash.

i know the world is too much

so if it's the smooth bowls with green stripe

you can have them

because the world will ask for more

itchy tags

bright lights

strong smells

always with the busy noise

a million cuts with vinegar and salt

from all the little knife stabs

of the world pressing in

and everyone says

ignore it all

just push through

in every pain

and no one

taught us

to breathe

to stop

not just bend and rend

under the wheel of time

but make this world ours

as trees reach for the sun

and stand rooted

on their own time

~ Krista Greene
Blog: sciencedragonwrites

ME/CFS: Definition, Symptoms, Prognosis

What is ME (ME/CFS)?

Myalgic encephalomyelitis, formerly known as **chronic fatigue syndrome**, now commonly referred to as M.E. or ME/CFS, is a disabling and complex disease characterized by overwhelming fatigue after even mild exertion, cognitive dysfunction ("brain fog"), unrefreshing sleep, muscle weakness, pain, difficulty staying upright for long, and other symptoms such as food sensitivities and environmental sensitivities.

Symptoms often get worse after physical or mental activity or emotional stress. This (sometimes delayed) reaction to even mild exertion or anxiety is known as **post-exertional malaise (PEM),** which is the defining characteristic of ME/CFS.

According to the Mayo Clinic,

"Chronic fatigue syndrome involves extreme fatigue that worsens with physical or mental activity but doesn't improve with rest."

How Common is ME?

The World ME Alliance states:

"Between 17 and 30 million people are estimated to have ME across the world, or approximately 1 in every 250 people. However, over 84% of people with ME are thought to be undiagnosed."

Symptoms of ME/CFS

Symptoms of chronic fatigue syndrome can vary from person to person, and the severity of symptoms can fluctuate from day to day.
11

According to the World ME Alliance,

"ME can get worse after any activity. This hallmark symptom is known as post-exertional malaise (PEM). The ability of people with ME to do their usual activities is greatly lowered. At times, ME may confine them to bed. People with ME have overwhelming fatigue that is not improved by rest. They may not look ill."

The most common symptoms, according to the Centers for Disease Control (CDC) and the Mayo Clinic, are:

- Ongoing physical and mental fatigue
- PEM (post-exertional malaise, extreme exhaustion, or a crash) after exercise or exertion (physical, mental, or emotional)
- Problems with memory or thinking skills; difficulty focusing or concentrating
- Muscle weakness
- Dizziness that worsens with moving from lying down or sitting to standing (orthostatic intolerance)
- Muscle or joint pain
- Unrefreshing sleep

Other symptoms many experience

Sensitivity to:

- Bright light
- Loud sounds
- Strong scents
- Heat and cold
- Certain foods
- Certain medications

Also, some people experience:

12

- Headaches
- Sore throats
- Tender lymph nodes in the neck or armpits

Some Limitations of People with ME/CFS

According to the CDC, people with ME/CFS may not look ill. However:

- They are unable to function the same way they did before they became ill.
- ME/CFS changes people's ability to do daily tasks, like taking a shower or preparing a meal.
- ME/CFS often makes it hard to keep a job, go to school, and take part in family and social life.
- At least one in four ME/CFS patients Is bed- or house-bound for long periods during their illness.

Impact of ME/CFS

From the World ME Alliance: "For 95% of people with ME, it is a chronic, life-long illness. Just 5% make a full recovery. Daily activities become challenging, and even small amounts of exertion can lead to an increase in other symptoms.

"People with ME have a lower average quality of life than people with diabetes, multiple sclerosis, stroke or various cancers.

"Initial research suggests roughly 75% of people with ME are unable to work, and many rely on care."

Can anyone get ME/CFS? How long does it last?

According to the CDC,

- Anyone can get ME/CFS. While most common in people between 40 and 60 years old, the illness affects children, adolescents, and adults of all ages.

- More women are affected than men. [Other sources mention that more than 70% of those affected are women.]

- ME/CFS can last for years or decades and sometimes leads to serious disability.

- An estimated 836,000 to 2.5 million Americans suffer from ME/CFS.

- About 90% of people with ME/CFS haven't been diagnosed.

For information on the **Levels of Severity and Causes of ME/CFS**, see the chapters near the end of this book.

> About 90% of people with ME/CFS haven't been diagnosed.

Long COVID or Post-COVID-19 Syndrome

What is post-COVID-19 syndrome?

According to the Mayo Clinic,

"Post-COVID-19 syndrome involves a variety of new, returning or ongoing symptoms that people experience more than four weeks after getting COVID-19. In some people, post-COVID-19 syndrome lasts months or years or causes disability."

What are the symptoms of post-COVID-19 syndrome (long COVID)?

Many of the symptoms are similar to the symptoms of ME/CFS.

The most common symptoms are:

- Fatigue
- Worsening symptoms after physical or mental effort —post-exertional malaise (PEM)
- Fever
- Respiratory symptoms, including difficulty breathing or shortness of breath and cough

Other possible symptoms include:

- Difficulty thinking or concentrating ("brain fog")
- Headache
- Digestive problems
- Dizziness when standing (orthostatic intolerance)
- Sleep problems

- Loss of smell or taste

- Depression or anxiety

- Joint or muscle pain

- Heart symptoms or conditions, including chest pain and fast or pounding heartbeat

The Mayo Clinic cautions, "Keep in mind that it can be hard to tell if you are having symptoms due to COVID-19 or another cause, such as a preexisting medical condition."

They conclude, "It's also not clear if post-COVID-19 syndrome is new and unique to COVID-19. **Some symptoms [of long COVID] are similar to those caused by chronic fatigue syndrome** and other chronic illnesses that develop after infections. Chronic fatigue syndrome involves extreme fatigue that worsens with physical or mental activity but doesn't improve with rest."

Post-Exertional Malaise (PEM)

What is PEM?

According to the Centers for Disease Control (CDC), "**Post-exertional malaise** (PEM) is the worsening of symptoms after even minor physical, mental or emotional exertion. ... People with ME/CFS often describe this PEM experience as a 'crash,' 'relapse,' or 'collapse.'"

Does it hit you right away? How long does it last?

The symptoms typically get worse 12 to 48 hours after the activity or exposure. In other words, you may be fine the day after overexertion, then it will hit you the following day, or even two days later.

PEM can last for days, weeks, months, or even years, depending on the severity of the exertion.

What are some of the symptoms of PEM (Post-exertional malaise)?

According to both the CDC and the Bateman Horne Center, symptoms may include:

- Debilitating fatigue
- Muscle weakness
- Difficulty thinking and concentrating ("brain fog")
- Problems sleeping
- Gastrointestinal difficulties
- Muscle and joint pain
- Sore throat
- Headache

17

- Dizziness

- Fever

- Chills

- Enlarged lymph nodes

- Increased sensitivity to noise, bright light, and odors

- Mobility problems ("wobbliness", weak legs)

Sometimes patients may be housebound or even completely bedbound during crashes.

According to the "Crash Survival Guide" published by the Bateman Horne Center,

"Once in a crash, the individual *must* allow their body to recover before resuming activities. It is critical to allow restoration and to avoid a repetitive push-crash cycle."

This is critical. They add, in bolded italics,

It is important to understand that crashes harm the body. Repeated crash sequences will threaten an individual's ability to return to their former baseline function, worsen or expedite harmful disease processes, and hinder the recovery process.

- ME/CFS CRASH SURVIVAL GUIDE, 2022

(Permission granted from the Bateman Horne Center.)

Pacing is Critical

If you have ME/CFS, long COVID, fibromyalgia, or any other condition causing fatigue, muscle weakness, and difficulty focusing, it's extremely important to:

Pay attention to your body and never push yourself beyond your current "energy envelope."

Pressing yourself to keep going when you're fatigued will almost always cause a crash (post-exertional malaise, or PEM) that could last from a day to several days, weeks, months, or even years, depending on how drastically you drove your body to continue when fatigued.

What is Pacing?

Pacing is the most important strategy for managing the symptoms of energy-limiting chronic conditions.

It's about taking a balanced, steady approach and managing your daily and weekly activities to avoid overdoing it and crashing or relapsing.

Pacing means being constantly aware of your physical, cognitive (mental), and emotional exertion, monitoring the intensity of your activities, and resting frequently throughout the day.

Pacing can help reduce the frequency or severity of flare-ups/crashes, where you would basically have to put your life on hold (or be forced to severely reduce productivity) until your energy returns.

Pacing refers not only to physical exertion but also to mental and emotional exertion.

It's critical to balance your daily physical and mental activities with regular relaxation and rest to avoid crashing.

The idea is to closely monitor your stress level and exertion (energy output) and replenish your reserves regularly through rest, so as not to overexert and end up in post-exertional malaise or a flare-up.

How to Pace Effectively

Learn to listen to your body.

Try to remember what happened the last time you exerted yourself or kept going when you should have stopped. Be constantly aware of what your body can take without getting worse.

Avoid stress.

It's critical to avoid stress as much as possible. When you're feeling tense, nervous, or anxious, try to find ways to calm yourself, like deep breathing, visualizing something or somewhere pleasant, spending time in nature, watching a relaxing or funny show, reading or listening to a good book, or working on a relaxing hobby.

Plan your daily activities and rest times.

Planning your day and week will help tremendously in reducing flare-ups because your body won't be stressed, wondering what's coming next, or being constantly driven.

Rest purposefully and frequently.

Set up mindful rests throughout your day.

Some examples: reclining (not lying flat) for 30–45 minutes after each meal to digest your food, taking a nap in the afternoon, and having sit-down or lie-down rests between or in the middle of tasks.

Rest "assertively."

For the most effective, replenishing rest, lie down or recline with no sound (using earplugs or noise-canceling headphones) in the dark or with an eye mask on. Don't engage in any input or activity. No checking your phone, reading, or watching TV. That will give you the deepest rest. Maybe listen to some quiet, relaxing, calming music. If you know how to meditate, that's probably even better.

Alternate busy days with rest days.

If you have a big activity, event, appointment, or visitors, don't houseclean, run errands, or go grocery shopping the day before. Have a quiet day to rest before the event or visitors. And plan a rest day or two afterward. Don't book anything on back-to-back days.

Don't overexert. Strive for moderation and consistency.

Build consistency into your planning to avoid the "push-crash cycle," or "boom and bust," where overexertion is followed by a crash (PEM), followed by recovery, more overexertion, and another crash.

The push-crash (boom and bust) cycle, where you push past your limits, then crash, is a harmful habit that can lead to long-term damage, where you would drop down a level and might not be able to return to your former baseline.

Be Kind to Yourself

When your energy is low
be good to yourself
don't make demands
just rest and recover

Do what you can
   little by little
Do something small
    then rest for a while
      then another small thing
       another rest
Pat yourself on the back
things will get done

When you feel low
list what you have done
even the little things

    got dressed
    had breakfast
    brushed teeth
    wiped the counter
    did a puzzle
    texted a friend
    avoided sugar

stopped

before you got too tired
and most important

rested and recharged

      ~ Jodie Renner

Keep Track of Your Heart Rate

To help pace yourself, use your heart rate as biofeedback.

When you're overexerting or stressed, your heart rate increases.

This is a reliable indicator that you need to slow down, relax, and take a break.

Without getting into too many details here, your goal is to mainly stay within your anaerobic threshold (safe heart rate level) to avoid overexertion, which could easily cause a crash/ PEM.

Our anaerobic thresholds vary, depending on our health, fitness level, and age. For those of us with limited energy, here's how to calculate your anaerobic threshold, which is the number of heartbeats per minute you want to stay below.

How to Calculate Your Safe Heart Rate Level

To find the number of heartbeats beats per minute without a smartwatch, you could find your pulse on your wrist or neck and count the number of beats in 15 seconds, then multiply that by four.

However, **the easiest and most accurate way to monitor your heart rate is to use a heart rate monitor or a smartwatch** (sports watch). See the information on smartwatches in the chapter, "Use Technology to Make Your Life Easier."

The Workwell Foundation (www.workwellfoundation.org) provides a reliable, easy method to use your heart rate to avoid overdoing it and causing PEM. Here is their procedure:

1. **Determine your resting heart rate (RHR).** Upon waking up in the morning, remain flat in bed and record your resting heart rate with an HRM (heart rate monitor, such as a smart watch). Do this every morning to calculate your 7-day average RHR.

2. **Use this average heart rate as a baseline** to calculate your safe heart rate doing activities. During activities, you heart rate should be no more than 15 beats per minute (bpm) above the RHR. This15 beats above your RHR is your anaerobic threshold.

3. **If your heart rate goes above your anaerobic threshold**, identify any activities and body positions (e.g., standing for too long) that put you over this HR. Workwell says, "Avoid spending more than 2 minutes above the anaerobic threshold."

4. **Learn to identify and recognize your symptoms** when you've gone above your HR threshold.

   Immediate symptoms may include difficulty breathing, dizziness, and nausea. Short- and long-term symptoms include muscle/joint pain, brain fog, headache, sleep disturbance, weakness, extreme fatigue, and more.

Workwell asks, "What is the first symptom you experience when over your threshold? This, plus heart rate, is a red-light indicator to stop activities before symptoms flare up."

5. **Rest until your heart rate returns to within 10 beats of your RHR.**

In their very useful guide, Workwell concludes:

If you "stay below the RHR+15 threshold and rest when the immediate symptoms of exceeding the anaerobic threshold occur, over time, short-term and long-term PEM symptoms will resolve."

So, in many ways, we are in charge of our recovery. If we monitor our heart rate and activities and follow the other protocols suggested by reputable websites and this book, we should slowly improve and be able to do more and more.

Another Way to Calculate
Your Safe Heart Rate Level

Here's another method to calculate your anaerobic threshold, the heart rate you should try to stay below:

Subtract your age from 220, then multiply the result by 0.6. (Or use 0.5 to be more conservative or if your symptoms are moderate or severe.)

Here's the formula:

(220 – age) x 0.6 (or 0.5)

So, for example, if you're 52: 220 – 52 = 168; 168 x .6 = 100.8 Round up to 101. (Or use 168 x .5 = 84)

Try to keep your heart rate below that number most of the time. If it goes up by 10 or more, sit down and relax for a while, or even lie down until it goes down.

Please consult your doctor or physiotherapist for more information on this formula and how to tailor it to your needs.

SET UP YOUR HOME TO MINIMIZE EFFORT

Simplify Your Living Space and Save Energy

Managing life with limited energy is challenging. Simplifying your home environment and handling tasks more efficiently can help conserve your energy and improve your overall well-being.

Let go of perfectionism.

Set up your home for convenience, not for show.

Forget about impressing guests or keeping up with the Joneses. Put your health first so you'll have more energy for essential activities and hopefully some enjoyable pursuits as well.

It's unlikely you'll be doing much entertaining, aside from family and close friends—at least not for a while. Give yourself a break and don't worry about not having a perfect show home.

34 Tips for Setting up a More Manageable Living Space and Organizing Chores

Simplify Your Living Space

Declutter: Remove most of the items you don't use or need that are cluttering up your home, to create a clean and organized living space. Sell, donate, or store the things you remove. Some things will of course stay because of their sentimental or aesthetic value, because they "spark joy." Keep those!

Simplify decor: Minimalist décor in relaxing colors can set the tone to create a calming atmosphere.

Prioritize rooms: Focus on organizing and simplifying frequently used rooms first. You could even designate rarely used rooms as "no-go" spaces, to save energy cleaning them.

Get rid of bulky furniture: Minimize furniture pieces to create open spaces and reduce obstacles. Try to sell big, heavy furniture online or donate to Habitat for Humanity, the Salvation Army, or another charity.

Keep (or replace with) lightweight, easy-to-clean furniture: Choose lightweight and easy-to-move furniture to simplify rearrangements. Opt for surfaces that are easy to clean to reduce maintenance effort.

Make furniture do double duty. Two examples would be an ottoman with storage inside and an end table with a shelf below.

Ensure comfortable seating: Invest in a few comfortable and supportive seating options. An office chair on wheels with good back support is a great option, with or without armrests. And I couldn't survive without my recliner! But an easy chair with a foot stool would be almost as good.

Eliminate or reduce chemicals and mold in your home. They are contributing to your malaise! See the next chapter.

Automate tasks to save energy: Use smart home devices to automate tasks like adjusting the thermostat or turning lights on and off.

Sensory-friendly spaces: Create a calming environment by adjusting lighting, sound, and temperature to your comfort.

Lighting: Use natural light when possible and look for adjustable lighting to control brightness.

Noise control: Use rugs, curtains, or soundproofing materials to control noise levels.

Temperature control: Ensure your living space is at a comfortable temperature to avoid additional stress. If this is out of your control, layer with clothes. See the chapter on surviving hot summer weather.

Organize essentials: Keep commonly used items within easy reach to minimize the need for excessive bending or reaching.

Set up smart storage: Use storage containers to keep similar items together so they'll be easier to find.

Use labels: Label shelving and large and small storage containers for easy identification.

Use task baskets: Use organizer baskets or totes to gather items needed for specific tasks (sewing, cleaning, crafts, etc.) to minimize trips around the house.

Create rest zones: Set up two or three areas for resting to avoid overdoing it. Beside each rest spot, put an end table or cart to set your hot or cold drink, tissues, glasses, phone, nail clippers, emery board, scissors, pen and pad, e-reader, tablet, passwords, and anything else you use often.

Hydration Stations: Place water bottles in convenient locations to stay hydrated without having to get up and go to the kitchen.

Mindful breathing spaces: Designate areas for mindful breathing exercises or meditation. Maybe an easy chair or a yoga mat on a carpet.

Assistive mobility devices: Leave canes in a few rooms, for times when you need one. You can also get cheap two-wheel walkers second-hand. Maybe have one in each of the main rooms you use. A rollator four-wheel walker in the kitchen would be handy to sit on while preparing food.

29

Energy-efficient appliances: If possible, invest in appliances that require minimal effort to operate. If you don't have a dishwasher, consider getting a portable countertop one.

Use adaptive tools: Invest in tools that make daily tasks easier, such as long-handled reachers or ergonomic tools.

Organize your computer files: Use digital tools for organizing schedules, reminders, and important information. Update and organize your digital files and documents to easily locate information.

Automate Tasks: Set up automation for repetitive tasks, such as bill payments or reminders. All my bills are automatically withdrawn from my bank account. Otherwise, I'd forget to pay them!

Comfortable Bedding: If your bed is old, look for a comfortable and supportive bed and breathable bedding to enhance the quality of your sleep.

Adaptive Clothing: Choose clothing that is comfortable and easy to put on, so you don't tire yourself out just getting dressed! (See the section "Clothing".)

Organize Your Daily Routine and Tasks to Save Energy

You have limited daily and weekly energy, and you don't want to use it all up on minor tasks. If you make the small, everyday chores easier, you'll have some energy left for activities you enjoy and want to do more often.

Daily Planner: Use a daily planner to remind you of tasks and to allocate your limited energy effectively.

Prioritize Tasks: Focus on essential tasks and prioritize them to conserve energy for critical activities.

Establish a Routine: Develop a daily routine that varies your activities and balances activity with rest.

Pacing: Practice pacing yourself by breaking tasks into smaller, manageable steps and taking breaks as needed.

Enlist help: Establish a support system for help with tasks that may be challenging. Don't hesitate to ask for assistance when needed and communicate your needs to others.

Online shopping: Use online shopping services with delivery to reduce the need for physical trips to stores. Or order groceries online for pickup.

Meal preparation: Plan simple and nutritious meals in advance to minimize energy spent in the kitchen. Use easy-to-prepare recipes. Or just have nutritious snacks and finger foods readily available.

Batch cooking: If you're able to cook or on good days, make a big pot of soup or stew or a favorite casserole and freeze portions to reduce the frequency of cooking.

Everyone's experience with ME/CFS is unique, so it's essential to tailor these suggestions to your own needs, preferences, and circumstances.

Effort Savers for Your Home

Here are some items to consider to make your life easier. (Not all of us can afford *all* of them, of course.) You may be able to find many of them second-hand or on sale.

NOTE: I don't endorse any particular brand of any of the products I mention anywhere in this book. Although I own some of them, I haven't tried them all. These are just suggestions for you to consider.

Be sure to check the reviews of any product. I never buy anything with a rating of less than 4.0 out of 5 stars, and I don't trust the ratings if there are fewer than 12 of them.

Recliner, chaise longue, sofa, or love seat

so you can relax leaning back and with your feet elevated. So important!

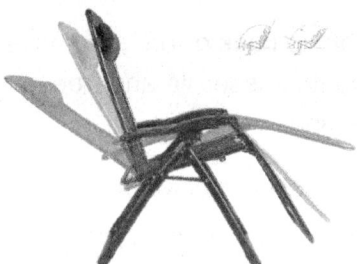

A zero-gravity chair is a lower-cost alternative to a recliner.

Lightweight upright vacuum cleaner

Both cordless and corded lightweight upright vacuums take much less energy to use than heavier upright vacuum cleaners.

Canister vacuum cleaners are also easier to maneuver than heavy upright ones.

Robot vacuum

A Roomba or other robot vacuum could keep your floors and carpets clean with no effort on your part.

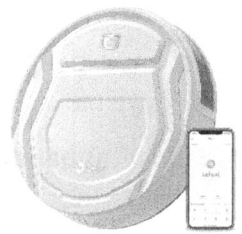

Long-handled cleaning tools

Use long-handled cleaning tools to reach high or low places without straining. Try a bathtub cleaner on a collapsible pole.

Electric spin scrubber

Look into a cordless electric spin scrubber with various heads for scrubbing different surfaces—shower, bath, sink, floors, windows—to save your energy.

Laundry basket on wheels

A laundry basket with wheels makes it so much easier to move clothes to and from the laundry room.

Grabber-reacher

They're indispensable for grabbing items that are too high or too low. The new ones are so much sturdier and work better than the older ones.

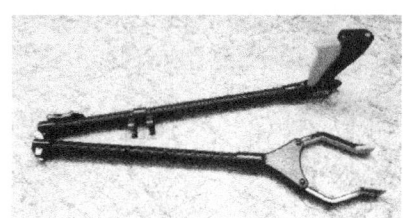

Freeze premade meals, microwave meals, frozen veggies and fruit, or portions of any big batches of food you find the energy to cook. No reaching down into a deepfreeze to dig out stuff.

Noise-canceling headphones to help muffle sounds so you can rest more calmly.

Collapsible wagon

Great for bringing groceries and other items to and from the car, taking out the trash and recycling, and transporting things from room to room. Mine is sturdy canvas on a metal frame, with four wheels and a handle. Folds up for easy storage. A real energy-saver!

Stool in closet to make it easier to reach items on the shelf along the top.

Laptop tray with a cushion bottom

for holding your laptop or tablet or craft project while on the sofa, in your easy chair, or in bed.

Automatic lights, motion-sensor lights, or smart light bulbs will save you getting up and save money on electricity.

Automatic pet feeders

If you have pets, use automatic feeders to reduce the effort required for feeding.

Lever door handles

Replace round doorknobs with lever-style handles for easier door opening.

Room air purifier (to eliminate smoke, pet dander, etc.)

Room air cooler or heater to help maintain a more comfortable body temperature

Portable, foldable utility cart

The one pictured here is called a "Pack-N-Roll". Light weight but strong, and folds up easily to store.

Essentials to Keep within Reach

To make your life easier and save precious energy, keep what you need close at hand. Or find an easy way to move your essentials wherever you go.

One idea is to gather the small items you use most in a basket with a handle or a cart on wheels to transport them from one room to another with you. Or, if you have a walker with a basket, you might choose to use that.

Another idea is to load a basket, tray, tote, or box with essentials for each of the two or three locations where you spend most of your time.

Some essentials to keep beside your sofa, easy chair, or recliner:

- Cup of tea or coffee

- Water

- TV remote

- Cellphone (mobile)

- Kindle e-reader

- Tablet (e.g., iPad)

- Tissues

- Neck pillow

- Sleep mask

- Earplugs

- Sunglasses (for when the light is too bright)

- Hat with brim (for the same reason)

- Small scissors

- Nail clipper

- Nail file

- Lip balm

- Flosser, floss sticks

- Eyeglass cleaner solution and cloth

- List of your passwords

On your bedside table

Suggestions for items to keep on, in, or near your bedside table:

- Drinking glass or water bottle with a straw

- Sleeping mask

- Ear plugs

- Flashlight

- Tissues

- Reading glasses

- Pen and paper

- Sleep aids

- Eye drops

- Sore throat lozenges

- Lip balm

- Hand lotion

- Phone

- Charging cord for phone

- Charging cord for smartwatch

I recently got two **3-tier utility carts** on wheels, one for beside my recliner and another for beside my bed. I'm so glad I did, as they both save me a lot of getting up to look for things.

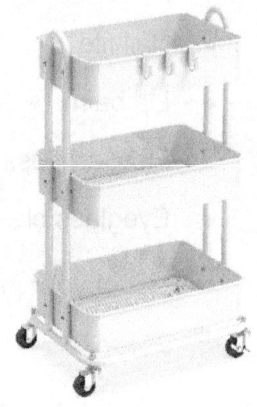

In the cart beside my recliner, I put hobby supplies, puzzle book, coloring book, my Kindle, tablet, scissors, pen, and paper—and anything else I want nearby.

If you can afford one, a smartwatch (sports watch) is on the list of essentials, too. See page 113.

Organize Your Kitchen to Save Time and Effort

Organizing your kitchen can help you conserve your energy when preparing food. Here are some ways to rearrange your workspace for optimum convenience.

Make sure all essentials are within easy reach.

Declutter.

Start by decluttering your kitchen. Get rid of (put away, sell, or give away) small appliances and other items you rarely use and keep only the essentials handy. This makes it easier to find what you need.

Reorganize your kitchen cupboards and shelves.

Move hard-to-reach items you use every day from the top and bottom shelves to middle shelves and countertops. Reserve the highest and lowest shelves for rarely used items. Keep whatever you use most within easy reach.

Forget the advice to have empty kitchen counters—use the countertop too.

To avoid expending unnecessary energy reaching down or up for things, keep the small appliances you use often—like your electric kettle, teapot, coffeemaker, toaster, and blender—close at hand on your counter.

Set up a sit-down work area.

Create a comfortable sitting area in the kitchen for tasks like chopping, peeling, or mixing. Use a sturdy chair or stool with proper back support.

Use lightweight, ergonomic cookware.

Opt for lightweight pots, pans, and utensils to make handling easier, and invest in ergonomic knives and other tools with comfortable grips.

Use adaptive tools.

Consider using adaptive tools like an electric can opener, jar openers, an electric immersion blender, easy-grip utensils, and other electric appliances to reduce manual effort. Explore kitchen gadgets designed for individuals with arthritis or mobility challenges.

Label shelves and drawers.

This is especially useful if you get help from others to clean your kitchen and/or unload your dishwasher.

Label containers:

Label containers in your pantry, fridge, and freezer to quickly identify ingredients. This helps prevent duplicate purchases and keeps everything in order.

Invest in clear containers.

Use clear containers for pantry, fridge, and freezer items, so you can easily see what you have. This prevents overbuying and helps you keep track of your supplies.

Group similar items together.

Keep similar items together in the pantry, refrigerator, and freezer. Grouping items by category makes it easier to find and access what you need.

Consider using lazy Susans or turntables.

in your fridge or cupboards to rotate condiments, spices, etc. for easy accessibility.

Rotate stock.

Practice the "first in, first out" rule in your pantry. Place newer items at the back and older items at the front, ensuring that you use up older ingredients before they expire.

Use drawer dividers.

Organize utensils and kitchen tools using drawer dividers. This keeps items separated, making it easy to find what you need quickly.

Store pans vertically.

Use vertical storage solutions for your frying pans, baking pans, and cutting boards to save cabinet space and make them easily accessible. You can find metal dividers originally meant for files, records, or CDs at thrift stores.

Maximize vertical space in cabinets.

Install shelves or organizers to make use of vertical space in cabinets. This helps you store more items without cluttering the countertop.

Organize with baskets and bins.

Use baskets or bins to corral smaller items in the pantry or cabinets. This makes it easy to pull out a group of items instead of searching through the entire space.

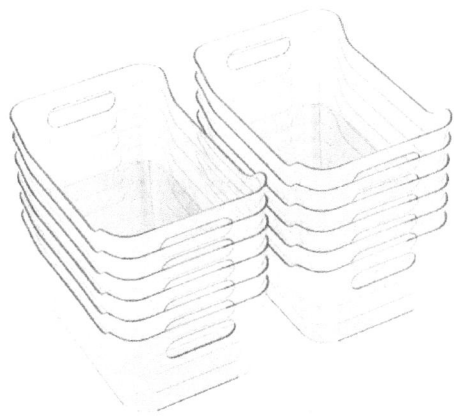

Install pull-out shelves.

If possible, have pull-out shelves installed in cabinets to make reaching items at the back easier. This maximizes storage space and ensures nothing gets lost in the depths of your cabinets.

Create a meal planning station.

Designate an area for meal planning, with a bulletin board or a magnetic board for recipes, shopping lists, and a weekly meal plan. This centralizes information and reduces search time.

Delegate tasks.

Enlist the help of family members, others in the household, or friends for tasks that require more energy. Emphasize the need for communication and collaboration in buying food and preparing meals.

Bottom line:

By setting up handy seating, easily accessible appliances, tools, and ingredients, and labeled shelves and drawers, you can create a user-friendly kitchen space that will save you and others time and effort preparing meals.

Of course, be sure to adapt your kitchen environment to your own specific needs.

Plan ahead, listen to your body, pace yourself, and don't hesitate to ask for assistance when needed.

Energy-Saving Aids for Your Kitchen

Small Appliances and Gadgets for the Kitchen

You can find many of these small appliances pre-owned at thrift stores or on Facebook Marketplace or other online second-hand sites.

Must-haves for conserving your energy:

- Microwave oven

- Blender for smoothies, soups, etc.

- Hand immersion blender for soups, etc.

- Slow cooker (often available at second-hand stores)

- Electric kettle – boils water quickly without the need for constant monitoring

- Jar opener (various types available)

- Ergonomic kitchen tools: utensils with large, comfortable grips and easy-to-use designs, reducing strain on the hands and wrists.

- Adaptive cutting board – with a non-slip base. Or just put a damp dish towel under it to keep it from moving.

Helpful wish-list items to save effort in the kitchen:

- Air fryer

- Instant cooker

- Stand mixer

- Food processor

- Vegetable chopper

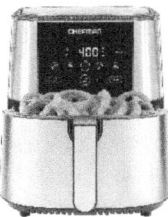

- Electric knife

- Silicone baking mat, muffin tin, etc.

- Toaster oven

- Electric can opener

- Nut and seed grinder (coffee grinder)

- Knife sharpener

- Mixing bowls with non-slip bases and easy-pour spouts

- Rice cooker

- Egg cooker

- Under-cabinet jar opener

- Anti-fatigue, non-slip floor mat

- Perching stool or kitchen stool

- Countertop dishwasher (to eliminate bending and lifting). Portable ones, with no water hookup needed, start at $300 (maybe less on sale). You can fill its water tank from the faucet or by hand and drain it into your sink or a bucket.

Safety and Mobility Aids for the Bathroom and Bedroom

Here are some suggestions for products that could help conserve your precious energy and ease your aches and pains. I have some of these aids and have found they make a huge difference in my energy and comfort levels.

Bathroom:

Shower chair or stool

Showering can be exhausting. Sitting on a chair will definitely reduce the effort a shower takes. Essential for those of us with orthostatic intolerance or POTS.

Stool for perching on to brush teeth, etc.

Rubber mat for floor of bathtub or shower

Safety grab bar for bathtub (image)

Grab pole for bathtub or shower

(image) I love mine.

Bath lift chair for bathtub

Grab bar for wall of shower or near toilet

Toilet support frame

(several varieties available)

Bedroom:

Wedge pillows are useful for raising your head and shoulders or feet and legs. They are a low-cost way to make yourself more comfortable if you're couch ridden or bedbound, or even for daily rests. The last thing you need is more pain from your positioning.

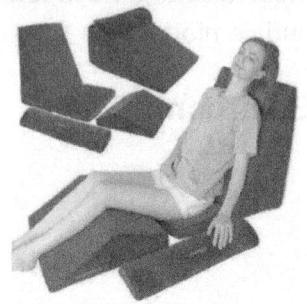

Knee and body pillows are very useful for decreasing pain and increasing your overall comfort. Some people find a pregnancy body pillow helpful for aches and pains.

Eye mask and earplugs

To improve your sleep, get a large, good-quality, cotton Velcro eye mask, which stays on better than the dollar store ones and is cooler and softer. It completely blocks out light.

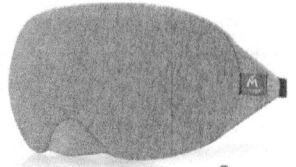 

The loop-style earplugs are highly recommended but kind of pricey. There's a good variety of earplugs to choose from on Amazon. The ones pictured above work well for me. I just trim down the "stick" to an optimal length.

For the bedbound:

Consider a **bedside commode** or a portable female or male **urinal**. They both come with a lid.

There's a good variety of **bedpan**s available now too.

Bedside aids

To increase your comfort and safety, consider some of these:

Bedside table organizer for phone, glasses, and hygiene essentials

Bedside lamp with adjustable brightness, preferably with touch turn on and off

Bedside caddy for your phone, tablet, pen, and paper

Bedside cart. A rolling 3-tiered utility cart works great for your snacks, drinks, bed socks, hobbies, and more.

Bed table for eating, working on hobbies, and playing games while in bed.

Bed support grab bar to help with getting out of bed.

Adjustable bed. If you're forced to spend a lot of time in bed, consider saving up for an adjustable bed, which will easily and smoothly rise and lower at both the head and feet (or one or the other) with a remote. The twin bed size is much more affordable.

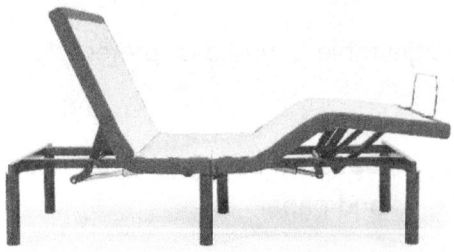

Laptop stand, angled to support your device while you're propped up in bed, or a laptop desk that swings over from your bedside table

Here's a photo of my "second office," in my guest room. I find this arrangement much less tiring than sitting upright at my computer.

Streamline Your Clothing

Dress for comfort—not couture–and limit your clothing.

Don't feel bad about hanging out at home in your PJs or sweats. Focus on more comfort and less energy spent!

Choose three or four (or five or six) favorite comfortable outfits for each season and make them easily available (like hanging on the outside of your closet door) to save the energy you would spend trying to choose what to wear each day.

As a woman, I like comfortable, casual house dresses (with or without sleeves) with pockets for summer, and for winter, long tunic tops with leggings or a warm, fuzzy robe for around the house.

Wear clothing with pockets.

Pockets in every outfit—the bigger, the better—will save you steps and effort when carrying things from room to room. (It's important to keep your cellphone with you.) Men usually don't have to think about this, but women's clothes often lack pockets. Ladies, don't buy any more pants, shorts, skirts, or dresses without pockets! Front or side pockets are best, of course. And deep pockets will prevent things from falling out when you're sitting down.

For colder weather, instead of a sweater or sweatshirt without pockets, choose a hoodie with a large kangaroo pouch in the middle. It's so convenient for storing your cellphone, glasses, tissues, and other small essentials.

In warmer seasons, add a vest or cardigan with pockets over your T-shirt. Or throw on an apron or a smock with pockets, or a cross-body bag or pouch.

12 More Clothing Tips for People with Limited Energy and Mobility Issues

To save time and effort, choose clothing with these features/characteristics:

Comfortable fabrics

Opt for soft, breathable fabrics like cotton or jersey that are gentle on the skin and easy to put on and take off.

Loose fitting

Loose-fitting clothes are generally more comfortable and easier to put on. Avoid tight cuffs, collars, or waistbands that may be difficult to manage.

Layered clothing

Dressing in layers allows for easier adjustments on and off when the temperature (or your internal temperature) changes.

Open-front cardigans or jackets

They make layering simpler and are often easier to put on than hauling clothes over your head, providing warmth without the struggle.

Elastic or drawstring waistbands

Clothing with elastic or drawstring waistbands can be more comfortable and easier to manage than regular waistbands with buttons and zippers. And forget belts.

Or avoid waistbands. If you're a woman, comfy dresses or robes are a good option.

Front-closing bras

Bras with front closures are easier to put on and take off compared to those with back closures. Look for bras with soft materials for added comfort. Sports, yoga, or sleep bras are usually more comfortable. Or no bra at all!

Zippers or ties/sashes

Often easier to manage than buttons or snaps.

Larger buttons

If buttons are necessary, opt for larger ones, which are easier to handle for those with limited dexterity.

Adaptive clothing

You might want to look for clothing with Velcro or magnetic closures instead of buttons or snaps, as they require less dexterity and effort. Do a search for "adaptive clothing" on Amazon or other online sites for more styles and features.

Slip-on shoes

Choose shoes that can be easily slipped on, such as slippers, clogs, sandals, open-back sneakers, loafers, or sneakers with elastic laces. Avoid shoes or boots with complicated buckles or laces.

Adaptive accessories

Accessories like a long-handled shoehorn or a device to help put socks on can make dressing quicker and easier.

Always remember that comfort is key, and there's no one-size-fits-all solution. Choose clothing based on your own preferences and needs.

You may even consider consulting with an occupational therapist for more personalized clothing recommendations.

Personal Care Energy Savers

Here are some items to consider that should help reduce pain or discomfort, relax your muscles, and save your valuable energy, especially if you're in a crash.

Again, I don't endorse any specific products or brands. These are just suggestions for you to look into.

Soothing eye mask that can be heated in the microwave

Migraine cap – cools the head, so not just for migraines

Hand-held scalp massager

Electric heated blanket

Weighted blanket

Foot massager – several varieties available

Electric hand massager (image)

Hand warmer mitts (heat in microwave)

Compression gloves for arthritis

Massage mat to relax muscle tension, improve circulation and help with relaxation – lots of varieties available.

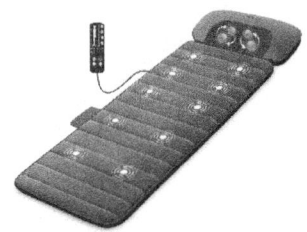

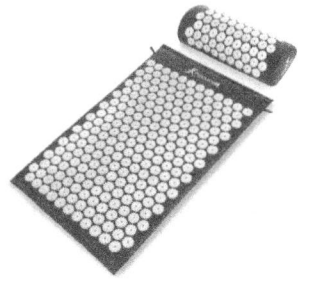

Acupressure mat for muscle relaxation and stress relief

Grounding ("earthing") sheet or mat

TENS EMS muscle stimulator for pain-relief therapy

Heated back and neck massager for a recliner or easy chair

Heating pad for neck and shoulders

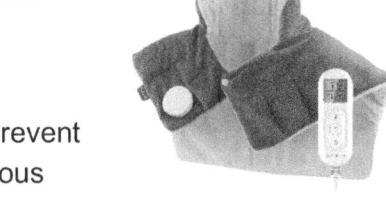

Tablet or cell phone holder to prevent fatigue of hands and wrists – various styles available

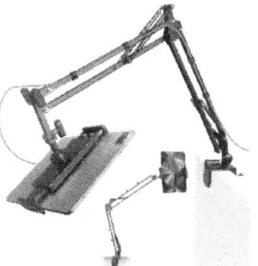

Personal Hygiene Aids

When you don't have the strength to shower or wash your hair, try these:

No-rinse, hypoallergenic, **body cleaning wipes**. Baby wipes are cheaper and work well.

No-rinse **body cleaning liquid** to use with a washcloth

Peri bottle for personal hygiene. Just add tap water at a temperature you like and squeeze to cleanse your privates while sitting on the toilet.

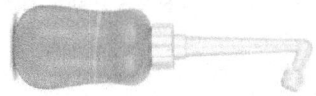

No-rinse shampoo. Simply apply (to dry hair), lather, and towel dry.

Dry shampoo. Comes in powder or spray. Or just use cornstarch or arrowroot powder. Google how to use it.

Dry shampoo cap with the shampoo inside. Great for those who are bed-bound.

Bidet-like attachment for your toilet – easier than wiping and will save you a lot of money on toilet paper. Water comes from the toilet tank. More expensive ones heat the water.

Decluttering Tips

Do you, like me, have too much stuff? Clothes that no longer fit, are uncomfortable, or don't work for your current lifestyle? Do you have files of papers that need to be thinned or things you no longer use but are still taking up space? Is it hard to find things you need because of all the other stuff in the way?

Decluttering can be challenging for anyone, but it can feel almost overwhelming for those of us with chronic low energy.

Here are some tips that should help you make the process more manageable.

Set realistic goals.

Don't get overambitious and empty out your clothes closet and dump all the clothes on your bed! Just looking at them will overwhelm and exhaust you. And you won't have the energy to sort them or put them back in the closet.

Instead, to avoid feeling overwhelmed, start small and break your decluttering tasks into manageable chunks. Focus on one area at a time, like a countertop, a drawer, or a cupboard or closet shelf.

Make a schedule.

Maybe pencil in days and times to devote to decluttering, for example, half an hour once or twice a week. If life or a crash gets in the way, pencil in a new time.

Gather supplies.

Before you begin, gather some boxes and trash bags, so you don't have to interrupt your work.

If possible, ask a friend or family member to assist you. Having someone else there can hopefully provide motivation and support.

Use the "four-box" method.

Label four boxes as Keep, Donate, Trash, and Sell (or Unsure). Place items in their respective boxes as you go through your belongings.

Prioritize safety.

Start with areas that pose safety hazards, such as cluttered walkways that create trip hazards. Then tackle high-traffic or high-clutter areas. This approach will give you the most immediate benefit and satisfaction.

Declutter in batches.

Sort items into categories (e.g., clothes, cookware, books, electronics) and focus on one category at a time. This makes decision-making easier.

Move drawers and boxes to somewhere you can sit.

Or get someone to do this for you, so you can sit in comfort while you're sorting and decision-making. I move cluttered drawers and files to my coffee table and sit on the couch. I can spread items to either side of me on the sofa: keep, toss, recycle, shred.

Use a timer.

Set a timer for short intervals (e.g., 10–30 minutes, depending on your energy level) and work on decluttering during that time. When the timer goes off, stop and take a break of at least 10 minutes—or quit for the day.

Declutter one area at a time.

To avoid getting overwhelmed, focus on decluttering one room or one area within a room until it's clean. That will also give you more satisfaction than making small dents in the clutter in various rooms.

Triage your clothes and shoes.

Keep only clothing that fits comfortably and is appropriate for your current lifestyle. Donate, sell, or trash items you no longer wear.

Make quick decisions.

Try to decide quickly about what to do with each item. If you haven't used or needed it in the past year, consider letting it go.

Reward yourself.

Set up small rewards for yourself after completing specific decluttering tasks. This can motivate you to keep going or to continue on another day.

Save photos of your sentimental items.

When dealing with sentimental items and those souvenirs from trips, consider taking photos (at least of the larger, bulkier items) and make an album or scrapbook to preserve the memories without keeping all the physical memorabilia.

Digitize your paperwork.

Scan important documents and reduce paper clutter by keeping digital copies on a secure computer or cloud storage. For safety, be sure to shred any paperwork with your name and other sensitive information, rather than just tossing or recycling it.

Clean up your old computer files too.

Go crazy with the "delete" button (trashcan image) on your old computer files and emails. If needed, seek assistance with decluttering your computer, tablet, and/or smartphone, so they'll run more efficiently and securely.

Streamline your kitchen.

Keep only essential cookware, utensils, and dishes. Donate, give away, or sell items you no longer need.

Organize your bathroom.

Get rid of expired toiletries and makeup and keep only your current necessities. Check the "best before" dates on your health-related supplies and meds and dispose of expired medications safely.

Evaluate your furniture.

Do you need all your furniture pieces? Are some things in the way, impeding your movement, or causing safety hazards? Consider multi-functional furniture to create more space.

Schedule regular decluttering sessions.

Establish a routine for decluttering, such as once a week or month, to prevent more clutter from accumulating.

Use the "one in, one out" rule.

To maintain a clutter-free environment, for every new item you bring into your home, consider removing one similar item.

Take your time and pace yourself.

If, like me, you have a lot of clutter (too much stuff!), remember that decluttering is a marathon, not a sprint. And a marathon that takes days, weeks, or months, with many rest breaks built in along the way. If you overtire yourself during one decluttering session, you're unlikely to attack the clutter again anytime soon.

Gradual progress is still progress.

The goal is to, without overexerting yourself, create a more peaceful and organized living space that supports your well-being rather than impeding it. Good luck!

Purge Chemical Products from Your Home

Many of us are sensitive to strong scents, especially chemical odors.

Chemicals in our environment can often cause us distress.

People with energy-limiting chronic conditions and sensitive nervous systems can experience mild to severe allergic reactions from smelling, inhaling, or using:

- Household cleaners and chemicals
- Scented beauty and personal hygiene products
- Glues
- Perfumes and colognes
- Inks and dyes
- Cigarette smoke
- New carpets or sofas off-gassing
- Automobile exhaust and diesel fumes

Symptoms include:

Headaches, dizziness, faintness, nausea, and stomach upset.

Be Proactive.

If you experience any of the above symptoms when exposed to chemical products in your home or workplace, replace those products.

> Ask people not to use perfume or cologne around you and to refrain from smoking in or near your home.

Use Safe, Scent-Free Products.

Use scent-free, hypoallergenic personal care products such as skin lotions, wet wipes, soaps, and deodorant.

Stop using dryer sheets and fabric softeners. The chemicals in them are very likely causing your body stress.

Replace any toxic household and garden products with more natural cleaners, detergents, and pesticides.

Try these environmentally safe cleaners that save you money and do the job:

Earth-Friendly Cleaning Solutions

White vinegar and baking soda are two safe and effective cleaners for your home. Add a few drops of an eco-friendly dish soap such as Dropps power dish spray or Cleancut dish soap and some white vinegar to a bucket of water for an easy, natural floor cleaner.

To clean your kitchen counters and bathroom, fill spray bottles with an environmentally friendly all-purpose cleaner, like white vinegar and an eco-friendly dish detergent (two to three parts vinegar to one part detergent). Use full strength or dilute with water. Have one in the kitchen and one in the bathroom (or each bathroom).

Here's a good homemade all-purpose cleaner to add to a spray bottle, from keeperofthehome.org:

Homemade All-Purpose Cleaner

- 1/2 cup white vinegar
- 2 Tbsp baking soda
- 10 drops tea tree, lavender, or lemon essential oil (for their disinfectant properties)

Mix the vinegar, essential oils, and a little water before adding baking soda in a clean spray bottle (glass is best, about 12 oz.). Then fill to the top with water. Gently shake to mix ingredients, and then spray the surface, wipe with a cloth, and allow it to dry.

How to Unclog Your Kitchen Sink without Chemicals

Is your kitchen sink clogged up? Get out your white vinegar and large box of baking soda. Pour about a cup of baking soda down the drain first, then pour about one cup of white vinegar down the drain as well.

Cover it and let the two ingredients sit in the sink for 15 to 20 minutes. Boil a kettle full of water and pour it down the drain to finish clearing it out.

Voilà! Sink is cleared, with no harsh chemicals used.

Mold in your home or environment can cause respiratory problems and other health issues. Be sure to get your home tested for mold!

CONSERVE YOUR DAILY
ALLOTMENT OF ENERGY

How to Make Daily Tasks Less Onerous

Are everyday tasks stealing all your energy or making you feel overwhelmed? Are you berating yourself because you can't accomplish what you used to be able to around home?

First, let go of perfectionism! It's just not worth it.

Put your health before a perfect, spotless home!

I'll help you figure out ways to accomplish necessary chores while conserving some energy for more enjoyable activities.

When (or before) the mess and clutter start getting you down, rethink your cleaning habits and strategies. Break down cleaning and housekeeping tasks into more doable chunks and use tools that will make them easier.

Housekeeping Hacks to Minimize Strain

Here are 30 suggestions for easing your workload when dealing with daily or weekly tasks.

Set Up Your Home to Save Your Energy

Declutter your common spaces.

Remove unnecessary items from living spaces to reduce the need for constant cleaning, avoid tripping hazards, and make navigation easier, especially for those who need to use a mobility aid.

Opt for minimalist decor.

Choose a minimalist approach to home decor to reduce the number of items that need dusting and cleaning. Fewer pieces of furniture will also make more space if you sometimes need to use a walker or wheelchair. And put away those knickknacks to make dusting easier.

Use non-slip mats.

Place non-slip mats in high-traffic areas, especially in the bathroom and kitchen, to prevent slips and falls.

Establish "no-go" zones.

Identify areas of the house that can be designated as "no-go" zones to reduce the space that needs regular cleaning. If you have a family room, a no-go zone could be your living room. If you have more than one bathroom, discourage use of the least convenient one.

Regular Maintenance:

Schedule routine maintenance to address any home issues promptly. This prevents the accumulation of tasks and ensures a manageable workload.

Organize essentials: Keep commonly used items within easy reach to minimize bending or reaching. Place frequently used items in easily accessible bins, drawers, and cupboards.

Label shelves and drawers: Label drawers and containers clearly to make it easier to locate items. Large, legible labels can help you and others identify things quickly. Consider getting a label-maker.

Make laundry more accessible: Get a laundry basket on wheels that you can pull, rather than lifting. (better yet, get two smaller ones for easier sorting).

Some suggestions to consider if/as your budget allows:

Keep an eye out for adaptive furniture:

Consider furniture with built-in storage solutions, such as ottomans with storage compartments, end tables with storage below, or beds with drawers, to minimize clutter.

Adopt low-maintenance materials.

Choose simple, easy-clean materials for furniture and home decor. For example, a solid surface is easier to clean than wicker or rattan.

Embrace technology.

If possible, invest in a robotic vacuum cleaner; an electric floor, window, and shower scrubber; or other smart home devices to make cleaning tasks easier.

Install task lighting:

Install additional lighting under your kitchen cupboards or in other work areas to improve visibility.

Install remote control outlets:

Use remote control or voice control outlets for lamps and other electrical devices, so you can turn them on and off without the need to bend or stretch.

Consider home automation:

Explore home automation options, such as smart thermostats, lights, and security systems, to simplify daily tasks and enhance energy efficiency.

Set up an emergency response system:

Consider installing an emergency response system to call for help in case of accidents or emergencies.

Plan Ahead to Save Energy

Prioritize tasks.

Identify the most essential tasks and focus on those first.

Create a schedule.

To avoid feeling overwhelmed and discouraged, develop a daily or weekly cleaning schedule to distribute tasks evenly.

Set realistic goals.

Break tasks into smaller, manageable goals, and celebrate achievements to stay motivated. Instead of "Clean up the kitchen," make a goal "Empty the dishwasher" or "Clear off the counter."

Incorporate rest breaks.

Schedule breaks during cleaning sessions to avoid exhaustion. Pace yourself and rest as needed. Clean for 5 to 15 minutes, then rest for 10 to 60 minutes, depending on your energy level. Repeat or move on to another activity.

Sit while cleaning:

- Place a chair or stool in areas where you perform tasks like folding laundry or sorting items, so you can sit and conserve your energy.

- Use a chair with wheels to move around while dusting or cleaning, reducing the strain on joints and muscles.

Rotate tasks:

Break down larger cleaning tasks into smaller, more manageable chunks to avoid fatigue, and focus on one area at a time.

Don't carry your cleaning supplies around:

Organize a **cleaning caddy** with all the necessary supplies to minimize trips back and forth. This can include cleaning solutions, wipes, and tools. Or have a **cleaning supplies area** in the kitchen and one in the/each bathroom.

Create cleaning stations.

Place cleaning supplies strategically around the house to reduce the effort required to access them. Put cleaning materials under both the kitchen sink and the bathroom sink, for example.

Delegate responsibilities.

If possible, delegate tasks to family members, your partner or roommate, or close friends, or hire help for specific chores. Make it someone else's job to vacuum, for example, or to take out the trash and recycling, or empty the dishwasher. Those jobs can be real energy-drainers for people like us.

Distract yourself.

Listening to an audiobook, podcast, or your favorite music while working can make the task more enjoyable.

Organize Your Tools

Use lightweight cleaning tools.

To reduce muscle fatigue and physical strain, invest in lightweight cleaning tools and equipment. For example, opt for a lightweight vacuum cleaner.

Utilize adaptive tools.

Explore tools designed for people with limited mobility or energy, such as extended-reach grabbers, long-handled bathtub cleaners, long-handled dustpans, and dish cleaners with soap-filled handles.

Use reach extenders.

Invest in reach extenders or grabbers to access items on high shelves, low cabinets, or the floor to reduce bending down and reaching up.

Invest in an electric scrubber with various brush heads.

Keep an eye out for these on sale. They're great for cleaning the floor, bathtub, shower, sink, windows, and more!

Use multi-purpose cleaning products.

Streamline cleaning by using cleaning products that can handle various surfaces.

Microfiber cloths are great for cleaning without a lot of effort. They trap dust and dirt easily, reducing the need for excessive scrubbing. You can clean your windows with just a microfiber cloth and water.

Establish New Habits

Change "do it later" to "do some now."

Aim for and encourage putting items away immediately after use to avoid clutter buildup. (Of course, you may not always have the energy to do this.)

The "5-second rule"

Before leaving a room, if something can be cleaned or put away in 5 (or 10) seconds, do it now. Scrub off that plate and put it in the drying rack or dishwasher.

Take something with you.

When leaving a room, take at least one thing that shouldn't be in that room. Even better, take three things. Don't leave empty-handed.

Take things halfway.

If you have stairs, place things that need to go up or down into baskets at the top and bottom of the stairs. Encourage others to do the same. If you don't have stairs and don't have the energy to take something to another room, put it halfway for now (in a box or basket for that purpose), and take it the rest of the way the next time you go to that room.

Clean the bathroom gradually.

Clean the sink and counter one day and the toilet another day. Do harder jobs, like the bathtub or shower, less frequently. For the shower walls, spray with a chemical-free cleaner and let sit for a while. Rinse off later.

Change your bed sheets with less effort.

It's best to have a second pair of sheets to put on the bed right away. If you wait until the one set of sheets has gone through the washer and dryer, you'll probably be too tired to remake the bed. Or you might forget all about it and, when you go to bed, suddenly realize you have to make it first!

You could also ask someone to put on 2 or 3 fitted sheets for you at once; then you can just remove the top one to wash.

Experiment with easier ways to wash floors.

Instead of a mop and bucket, consider trying a floor Swiffer, a Bissell steam mop and cleaner, a cordless electric mop, a spin mop, or a manual spray mop.

Ask for help.

Don't hesitate to ask for assistance when needed. Friends, family, and neighbors may be willing to lend a hand.

Consider professional cleaning services.

If you can manage it financially, hire someone to clean your home (or parts of it) every two weeks or once a month. To save money, have them concentrate on essential but labor-intensive tasks, like cleaning the kitchen and bathroom(s), vacuuming, washing floors, and cleaning windows, rather than dusting, which is easy but time-consuming.

The cleaning person could also strip your bed, put the sheets in the washer, start it, then proceed with the cleaning. As soon as the washer stops, they could move the sheets to the dryer. Before they leave, they could take the sheets from the dryer and remake the bed.

Bottom line:

Adapting your living space, choosing easier tools, getting rid of clutter, lowering your standards a bit, enlisting help, and managing your time more mindfully can all significantly ease the challenges of housekeeping with limited energy.

Of course, tailor these hacks to your own needs and abilities. Also, be sure to seek assistance from caregivers, hired help, or family members when needed.

Problems and Solutions in the Kitchen

Problem: Don't have a dishwasher. Washing dishes and pots by hand is too tiring.

Solutions:

- Avoid scrubbing pots and pans by using parchment paper in your slow cooker and baking tins.

- If you have caked-on pots from the stove top, sprinkle in baking soda, add water, and soak them for a while first.

- Avoid washing bowls and plates by using parchment paper on them before adding the food. Just throw out the parchment paper afterward and put the dish back in the cupboard.

- If you're really exhausted or in a crash, consider using disposable dishes and cutlery.

- Consider saving up for a countertop dishwasher.

Problem: Standing up to work in the kitchen is too tiring.

Solutions:

- Use a tall stool for sitting on while cooking, baking, or doing dishes. Two ideas:
    - Ikea – Franklin folding bar stool
    - Drafting stool on wheels with back and footrest

- If you have a rollator walker, try sitting on the seat to work in the kitchen.

- Sit down at a table to chop vegetables, stir batter, read a recipe, etc.

Problem: Cutting up vegetables and meat is tiring.

Solutions:

- Sharpen your kitchen knives.

- Move your cutting board to the table and do the chopping sitting down.

- Buy a vegetable chopper.

Problem: Can't reach that can or bag on the top shelf of my cupboard.

Solutions:

- Use a grabber-reacher to get it down. The new ones are so much better than the ones they sold years ago. They're adjustable and bendable, have a strong grip, and can lift heavier objects securely.

- Get someone to help you rearrange your kitchen shelves so the things you use most are within easier reach.

Problem: Twisting off the lid of a pickle, mayonnaise, or jam jar takes way too much energy.

Solution: Use a bottle-cap opener to move around the jar lid, prying it up until you hear a pop. Now you can easily open the jar. Or purchase an electric jar opener that runs on batteries.

Problem: Twisting open a bottle cap drains energy.

Solution: Use pliers to open it.

Problem: Emptying the dishwasher is tiring and hard on the arms. And the bending down and reaching up can make me dizzy.

Solutions:

- Empty it in two to four shifts, sitting down in between.

- Leave the dishes and cutlery in there and, as needed, use them directly from there.

- Consider getting a countertop dishwasher.

- Avoid the dishwasher and limit your dishes to two of each item—cups, bowls, glasses, plates, etc.—and just wash those items by hand. Leave the rest in the cupboard.

- If you're in a crash or at a severe level, consider using biodegradable, compostable dishes and utensils.

Problem: No energy to shop for groceries.

Solution: Order groceries online for pickup or delivery.

Problem: Too tired to put away the groceries.

Solution: Put away anything that needs to go into the freezer or fridge right away. Put away the nonperishables gradually over the next several days, or just use them up gradually from the boxes or bags.

Problem: Too tired to clean up after the evening meal or before bed.

Solution: Delegate this task or rest for 30 to 60 minutes first. Then do a little, rest, and do a little more. Or set a timer to work for five or ten minutes. It's surprising how much you can get done in five minutes. Also, once you start, you may find you're on a roll and can continue for fifteen minutes.

Personal Hygiene Tips to Save Energy

In a crash, shower less often.

Many people with ME or fibromyalgia find showering exhausting, especially during a crash. A **bath** might feel easier. If you do feel you need a shower, be sure to use a **shower chair** (preferably one with a back).

Heat can be exhausting for many of us, so it might be best to adjust the water to warm or even lukewarm, not hot.

Other shower tips:

Have a terrycloth bathrobe ready, and, instead of toweling yourself off, put on the robe and go to bed for a rest. If it has a hood, you can also wash your hair in the shower and put the hood up to help dry it.

If showers are arduous and draining, use some alternatives.

For much easier cleansing, experiment with baby wipes or no-rinse bathing wipes and no-rinse cleansing liquids that you can use while sitting or in bed. You'll find a variety of them on Amazon and elsewhere. See "Personal Care Energy Savers" for more tips for easier personal hygiene.

Simplify your hair care.

If washing your hair is exhausting, consider getting a shorter haircut. Wash it less often. Use leave-in hair conditioner. Or try no-rinse shampoo, dry shampoo, or a dry shampoo cap.

74

Find easier ways to dry your hair.

Towel dry it or let the air dry it. If using a hair dryer, sit, bend over, and blow the hair dryer upward. That's easier on your arms.

Brush your teeth with less effort:

- Sit on a stool or the toilet seat to brush.

- Use an electric toothbrush.

- Just use a fluoride mouthwash in a pinch.

- Brush your teeth in bed with a small bowl of water.

- Keep some tooth-flossing sticks or little interdental brushes and a Sulcabrush beside your bed or easy chair as an alternative to getting up to brush your teeth. I like the GUM Proxabrush interdental brushes, which come in five sizes.

- Consider investing in an autobrush (https://tryautobrush.com/collections).

- You can even get pre-pasted waterless disposable toothbrushes for your bedside table that can be used without water.

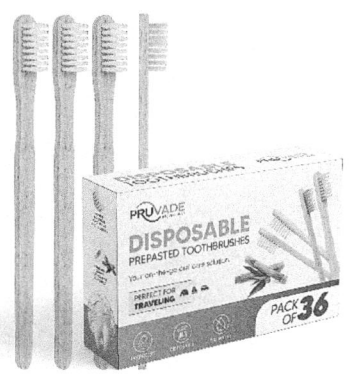

MANAGE YOUR DAILY "ENERGY ENVELOPE"

How to Avoid Draining Your "Body Battery"

Here are some essential guidelines for avoiding PEM/burnout and slowly improving your situation:

Accept Your Current Reality.

Acknowledge that your situation and abilities have changed (at least for now).

This one is difficult and takes time to accomplish. But not accepting your (new) limitations will only leave you frustrated, angry, and depressed—all of which will make you feel worse.

Recognize your reality and deal with it proactively.

Instead of dwelling on what you *can't* do, ask yourself, "What can I do to improve my situation and be able to do more?" It's important to be constantly mindful to stay calm and conserve your energy so you can last longer each day and have energy for enjoyable pursuits. Be sure to check on your body regularly. Do you feel fatigued? Tense? Overwhelmed? Practise positive self-talk and relaxation techniques.

Avoid comparing yourself to others.

Don't feel you need to keep up with friends of your own age or even those who are older. Accept where you are. Acknowledge what you can and can't do without exhausting yourself. Be kind to yourself and pay attention to your body. That will help you heal and hopefully improve.

Stay Calm. Don't Rush.

Avoid stress.

Stress drains energy more quickly than almost anything else. Try deep breathing, meditation, and gentle stretching. Or go sit outside on a nice day and focus on the nature around you. Listen to some relaxing music. If you're naturally nervous or hyperactive, anti-stress vitamins, herbal supplements, or prescribed meds may help.

Forget the urgency!

Except for actual life-or-death situations, learn to use calming self-talk, deep breathing, meditation, and other relaxation techniques (and maybe herbal supplements or meds) to convince yourself that the situation isn't as urgent as you think.

A fight-or-flight emotional and physical response will drain your energy extremely quickly, and you could be done for the rest of the day—or longer.

Avoid situations where you're forced to hurry.

If you're going out, get ready early so you don't have to rush. And don't walk out the door at the last minute. Leave early. This may be another habit you need to work into your life to change for your own survival. (I know I did.) Moving quickly and worrying about being late could tire you out fast. Then you might even have to cancel. Force yourself to slow down to conserve your energy. Breathe deeply while walking or driving to slow your heart down.

Keep hyperactivity and nervousness at bay.

See the chapter "How to Calm Your Nervous System" for ideas for relaxing.

Stop and Check in with Your Body Frequently.

Stay tuned in to your body.

Don't allow yourself to get overtired. When doing a task or even working on a hobby, check in with yourself frequently to see if you're getting fatigued. Be aware of your (new or recent) limits for any task. For example, where before you might have been able to work at the computer for an hour or more before taking a break, now you should aim for periods of 10 to 20 minutes, with rest breaks or moving around in between. Set a timer to remind you, if necessary, to avoid burnout.

When (or preferably before) you start to feel tired, take a break. Relax with your feet up in a recliner, an easy chair with a footstool, on your sofa, or in bed.

Keep track of your steps per day, and don't go too high.

Unlike athletes and fit people, people with energy-limiting conditions don't want to aim for 10,000 steps per day. In fact, that would very likely overtax our malfunctioning mitochondria and cause a crash or PEM. I try to keep my daily steps to between 1,500 and 3,500. Taking over 4,000 steps means I'm overexerting and might pay for it the next day. On days I can't reach 1,000 steps, I accept that, as they're most likely recovery days when rest is the number-one priority.

Keep your heart rate down.

Get a smartwatch that tells you your heart rate and check it frequently. (See the chapter on how to use a smartwatch to find your aerobic threshold.) If your heart rate is up, sit down and breathe deeply. If it's way up, recline or lie down until your HR goes down.

Beware of Overexertion!

Don't overexert yourself.

Exercise mindfully, don't rush, avoid lifting or carrying heavy things, and try to always stay as calm as possible.

Never push yourself to exhaustion!

This is so dangerous and can do long-term or even permanent damage. For many people with chronic fatigue, pushing through has resulted in them being bedbound for weeks, months, or even years. Besides physical overexertion, this also includes studying, writing, or other mental work. That goal or deadline you're stressing about is never worth it! The price you could easily pay is far too high.

Adrenaline is not your friend!

Beware of adrenaline. Like too much caffeine or sugar, it can make you think you have energy you really don't. Whether the situation is exciting and exhilarating or tense and scary, the sudden rush of (false) energy and pseudo strength that adrenaline gives you can make you forget to pace yourself and rest.

Overexerting can cause a serious, possibly long-term crash/setback/PEM. I know this only too well from personal experience. In my case, four days of high, positive adrenaline and overexertion on a trip caused a major crash that I still haven't completely recovered from a year and a half later.

Don't strain your brain.

Don't attempt difficult puzzles or sudoku, especially when you're tired. It will use up limited cognitive energy and be at the cost of your overall energy level. To relax, go for easy jigsaw puzzles, 500 pieces or fewer (I like 300 pieces) and easy crossword puzzles, word searches, and so on. I like solitaire because there's no pressure from other players, unlike a card game like bridge!

Plan Your Day and Week Wisely.

Check your calendar to avoid overcommitting.

Don't set up two or more commitments for the same day—spread them out. In fact, to avoid a "crash" and possibly getting worse, don't even plan appointments, shopping, outings, visitors, etc. for consecutive days. Plan a rest day or two in between to recover your energy. Some people can only go out once or twice a week for an hour or so. For others, it might be once or twice a month, or less.

Establish routines.

This reduces the need to constantly decide what to do, when, and how. Decision-making can be really draining. Break household jobs into smaller tasks that you can accomplish over a week or month. Add in some movement every day, such as stretching for 5 to 10 minutes, some chair yoga, or a short walk.

Don't get overambitious, or you'll pay for it later.

We just can't push ourselves anymore. It does too much damage, which can be permanent. Set lower goals, pace yourself, and rest frequently. A realistic goal for the day or week would be to do about half of what you think you can do and plan to do the rest of it in the days or weeks to come.

Find the easiest way to accomplish every task.

Work smart, not hard, to avoid wiping yourself out early in the day and having no energy left for the things you like to do.

Shop online and have your purchases delivered to your home. Don't deplete your body battery by trudging around big-box stores or malls.

Be methodical.

Think about the steps needed to carry out a task, then work on them methodically. Don't rush around willy-nilly. That will wipe you out so fast!

Don't multitask.

Change your habits. Don't do other things while having a phone conversation. Don't try to carry on a conversation and cook or bake at the same time. Turn off the radio or TV when working on the computer or reading a recipe. If you're driving, it's usually best to have the radio low or off. If you have a passenger, explain to them that you're no longer able to carry on a conversation while driving, as it's distracting and tires you out too much.

Change activities frequently.

If you've been working on the computer or doing paperwork, stop and walk around or lie down for a while. Or go outside. Sit on your balcony, deck, or porch, or in your yard or a nearby green space. Or put in a load of laundry, tidy up, or prepare some food. Change from exerting cognitive energy to using physical energy. And vice versa. With rests in between.

Include Planned, Deliberate Rests.

Take frequent rests throughout the day.

Make purposeful rests a part of your daily routine, even on days you feel better.

Our rests differ from what "normal" people would call resting. Watching TV, scrolling on your phone or tablet, or reading won't usually give you as much rest as you need. They're more like light activities.

Ideally, to rest and rejuvenate, lie in a dark room with no noise or sounds. Try to slow your mind as well. I can rest well in my recliner with the back lowered and the footrest up, with a good-quality sleep mask covering my eyes and good-quality earplugs blocking out sound. Meditating is even more effective.

When working, set a timer.

This is especially important for a task you really want to get done. Give yourself 5 to 30 minutes (whatever you can manage without getting overtired) to work, then set a timer to rest after that period of time. Rest for half to two or three times as long as you spent working. For example, you may need to limit yourself to 15 minutes of working, followed by 45 minutes of rest.

Alternate physical tasks, cognitive tasks, and rest.

Set a timer for 20 minutes (or whatever length of time will keep you within your energy envelope). Spend 20 minutes on a physical task, such as cleaning or laundry, then rest for 10-30 minutes, then spend 20 minutes on a cognitive task, such as reading, writing, crossword puzzles, or paying bills, then rest for 10-30 (or more) minutes. If you have the time and energy, repeat the cycle.

Eat Healthfully and Hydrate Frequently.

Maintain a healthy diet.

Eat foods that provide vitamins, protein, complex carbohydrates, and healthy fats. Always keep nutritious snacks nearby. To keep your blood sugar from dropping, it's best to have a light meal or healthy snack every two to four hours.

Avoid sugar, junk food, and alcohol.

Sugar might give you a short high, but it will soon wear off and you'll feel worse than before you had the candy or cake. If you really want a sweet treat, it's much safer to have a small amount after a meal rather than on an empty stomach.

Stay hydrated.

If you start to feel thirsty, you're already dehydrated. Keep water beside you at your table, easy chair, bedside, or computer, and regularly take sips all day. You can buy flavored water drops or sachets or add lemon or lime slices to make it tastier. Herbal teas and clear broths count as water. Also, add some electrolytes to your water, especially when you're exhausted or in a crash.

See the section on nutrition for more information on healthful eating.

How to Avoid Fizzling Out by Noon

Wake up gradually and get up slowly.

If you're lucky enough not to have to hurry for any reason (I make all appointments for 10 a.m. or later), take your time waking up.

If you can, lie there for a while to gradually wake up and just think about your day and rest. (Our sleep is usually not refreshing, so resting while awake can be more refreshing.)

When you decide to get up, put your feet on the floor and sit there for at least 10 seconds. While you're sitting there, be sure to drink some water. (Always keep water at your bedside.)

Get up and move slowly to use the bathroom, then get dressed while sitting on your bed.

When you get to the kitchen, sit down for at least a minute or two before starting breakfast.

Stay calm. Don't hurry.

If you feel yourself getting anxious, use calming self-talk and deep breathing to soothe your nervous system. This is critical to safeguard your energy.

Don't skip breakfast.

Try to have something easy, like granola or muesli and milk; or granola, yogurt, and berries; or eggs and toast; or toast with peanut butter or other nut butter with sliced banana on top. Or take out from the fridge something that you've prepared in advance, like overnight oats, that big pot of cooked oatmeal (with added seeds and nuts for protein), egg muffins, or any leftovers that appeal to you.

When preparing breakfast and your coffee or tea, take your time and move slowly and methodically. Hurrying will drain your body battery quickly! I know this very well from experience. Check your heart rate frequently on your smartwatch, and if it's more than 10 points up, stop and sit for a few minutes before continuing.

Don't overeat, or it will tire you out too much.

Your body takes a lot of energy to digest food, so eat a moderate amount of nutritious, easy-to-digest food for breakfast (and any other meal). If your breakfast is harder to digest, like granola or muesli, consider taking a digestive enzyme or probiotics pill with it.

Take your time eating and take your vitamins and supplements with breakfast.

Rest while your food digests.

Many of us feel we need to rest after breakfast. Don't beat yourself up about this. All your body's limited energy is going toward digesting your breakfast. I find if I rest in my recliner with my feet up for 20 to 45 minutes after breakfast, I usually get enough energy to do something productive after that.

I also often have a midmorning power smoothie (see recipes), and that gives me a boost of energy. It's easy to digest, so it doesn't tax my digestive system and make me tired.

Some Survival Tasks to Do on Your Good Days

Caution: I can't stress enough that it's really important to pace yourself and have rest breaks, even on your good days, in order to avoid the PEM payback of ending up in bed for several days, a week, or more.

Some ideas to help you survive the bad days:

Make some hard-boiled eggs. Boil some eggs and refrigerate them for salads or sandwiches, or for on toast, melba toast, or rice cakes.

Order groceries, concentrating on nutritious food that won't spoil quickly (frozen vegetables and fruit) or healthy frozen dinners. Or buy fresh and freeze.

Cut up some vegetables to refrigerate or freeze, then later cook them quickly in the microwave or add to purchased soups, stews, chili, etc.

Make a big pot of soup or stew or a casserole in your slow cooker and freeze in portions.

Make a big sheet-pan meal in the oven or air fryer that will create leftovers.

Make some overnight oats. Prepare four or five days' worth of overnight oats in jars and refrigerate.

Cook 4–5 days' worth of oatmeal in a pot or slow cooker, and mix in any nuts and seeds you like, to add protein. I like chopped walnuts and sunflower seeds. You can also add raisins, currants, dried cranberries, or chopped apple. This keeps in the fridge for up to five days. When serving, I add blueberries and non-dairy milk. For added protein, stir in some Greek yogurt or nut butter.

Make no-bake energy bites or some healthy breakfast bars. See Recipes.

Bake healthy cookies or muffins. For cookies, I like oatmeal with walnuts and dark chocolate chips. For optimal health, reduce the sugar in recipes. Chopped dates, mashed banana, or applesauce work well to add some natural sweetness.

Change your bedsheets. It's best to have two sets of sheets so you don't have to strip the bed, run the sheets through the washer and dryer, and remake the bed all in the same day. Or maybe have someone put on two or three fitted sheets at once, so when you remove the top one, you'll have a clean one underneath.

Freeze bags of ingredients for healthy smoothies. Then you can later just dump the contents in a blender, add liquid or yogurt and protein powder, blend, and drink. My baggies contain frozen cherries and berries, frozen sliced banana, and frozen spinach or kale.

You can also blend banana, berries, and spinach to make a very thick smoothie, then freeze it in an ice-cube tray to pop out later.

If you have a large blender, make three to four days of smoothies at once and divide into jars. Drink one that day, leave one in the fridge for the next day, and freeze one or two.

But don't push yourself to do more than you should on a good day! Stop and rest before you're tired and save 20% of your energy for the next day.

"I Didn't Do That Much Today. Why Am I So Tired?"

When you feel overly tired with no obvious reason, ask yourself these questions:

– Did I overdo it yesterday or the day before?

Sometimes post-exertional malaise skips a day (or even two), then hits you, so it could be from overdoing it two days ago, even though yesterday you were fine.

– Did I sleep poorly last night?

If so, why? What can you do to have a better sleep tonight? (See the chapter, "Get a Better Night's Sleep.")

– Did I hurry to go somewhere or rush around at home and raise my heart rate?

Pay attention to the heart rate on your watch or heart rate monitor, and try to keep it at recommended levels.

– Did I have music or the TV on too loud, with too much action and loud noises?

Sensory overstimulation is very tiring for us.

– Did I spend too much time in the sun on a hot day?

Heat and bright light can be exhausting for many or most of us.

– Was I around perfume or chemical fumes?

Strong scents can be toxic for us and stress our system.

– Am I (or was I) stressed?

What can you do to de-stress? See the chapter, "Calm Your Nervous System."

– Did I lift and carry something too heavy?

Take care not to overexert. Find easier ways to accomplish tasks, like using a cart.

– Did I forget to eat something nutritious in the last few hours?

Have a healthy snack or meal.

– Did I forget to eat protein in the last few hours?

Have a protein snack, like a boiled egg, jerky, a handful of nuts, some peanut butter or other nut butter on a whole-grain cracker, an apple with cheese or nut butter, or some celery and hummus.

– Did I forget to include some fresh vegetables and fruit?

Apples, oranges, bananas, celery, and carrots make easy snacks. Or buy cut-up veggies or a bag of salad. Also, vegetable juice is a quick way to get some easily digestible vitamins.

– Did I eat too many sweets or drink alcohol?

To feel good consistently, cut way back on the sugar and alcohol.

– Am I dehydrated?

Did you forget to drink water or other clear liquids in the last hour or two? Have a glass of water immediately.

– Did I forget to drink some electrolytes?

I add coconut water to my smoothies for electrolytes.

– Did I neglect to have at least one significant rest today?

Or did you think scrolling your phone while listening to music was a good enough rest? (It's not.)

How to Recover from a Crash

Tips to Help Survive Post-Exertional Malaise (PEM), Also Called a Crash, Setback, Payback, or Flare-Up:

Sleep or rest in bed for 11 to 13 hours or more at night.

If you're able, after waking, try to spend 10 to 60 minutes just dozing and relaxing in bed before getting up. That rest time helps build up some energy.

Take one or two (or more) naps.

Try a mid-morning nap and a mid-afternoon nap. You may need to stay in bed for most of the day or go from bed to couch or recliner.

Rest often during the day.

Lie or recline in a dark, quiet place, or use an eye mask and earplugs or noise-canceling headphones. Add a warm blanket or heating pad if you need it and keep a glass or bottle of water nearby.

Try to zone out and clear your mind. Meditate if you know how, or think of something pleasant, or just concentrate on your breaths—in and out, in and out.

Rest your body and mind as much as you need to.

If it's all day, think of it as an investment in your energy envelope or body battery, so you'll have more energy tomorrow or in a few days.

Stay calm and move slowly and methodically.

Soothe your body. Say to yourself, "There's no rush," "Everything doesn't have to be perfect," "Take it easy. It's time to relax and heal."

Avoid sensory overload.

Depending on your level of severity, turn music, TV news, and shows down or off. Wear earplugs if necessary. Avoid bright light. Wear sunglasses and a hat, even indoors if it's bright. Avoid strong odors.

Avoid extreme temperatures.

Have layers of clothing close by to put on and take off as the temperature fluctuates. Stay in the shade on hot, sunny days.

Avoid caffeine.

Your body is in recovery mode, and stimulation will delay the recovery. Switch to decaf coffee, weak green tea, or herbal teas.

Avoid stress.

Avoid confrontations; don't read, watch, or listen to anything that will cause you stress; and warn family and friends that you're in a crash or unusually tired today.

Limit brainwork.

Put off attempting anything that places demands on your cognitive abilities, such as reading, emailing, texting, watching complicated shows, and making important decisions.

Avoid socializing.

Tell family and friends that you can't talk on the phone or in person for now and that it might take you a while to respond to texts. If someone calls, ask them to text you instead, or set a timer and let them know that when the timer goes off, you'll have to end the call.

Stay hydrated.

Drink plenty of water all day, as well as clear broths and herbal teas.

Drink some electrolytes.

There are a variety available in bottles or powder form. Or add lemon, honey, and a pinch of salt to hot or cold water.

Don't eat large or hard-to-digest meals.

The digesting will tax your energy too much. Have small meals and healthy snacks.

Sip some soup.

Soup is soothing and can be full of easy-to-digest nutrients. I avoid chicken, meat, and beans when I'm in a crash. Instead, I add one or more of the following to soup for added protein: a swirled-in egg, bone broth powder, nutritional yeast, and frozen peas.

Have some easily digestible protein.

Put protein powder in juice or a smoothie, have yogurt or an egg, or spread peanut butter or other nut butter on celery or on crackers, topped with banana slices.

Save energy cleaning up after meals.

Consider using paper plates, bowls, and cups while in a crash. Or use parchment paper on your regular plates and bowls. It works well with cooked foods, salads, yogurt, etc. Then throw away the parchment paper and just put the plate or bowl back in the cupboard.

Drink healthy smoothies.

This is easiest if you already have the ingredients on hand. Keep berries, banana slices or chunks, and spinach or kale in your freezer. Also, have on hand some protein powder and/or Greek yogurt and/or pumpkin or sunflower seeds to add to your smoothies.

Distract yourself with some easy listening, if you're able.

If you can focus on spoken words, listen to an audiobook instead of trying to read when you have difficulty concentrating. Or listen to gentle music or a relaxing, calming app or podcast. If even that's too much, silence is most restful.

Take some vitamins and supplements.

I find that a good multivitamin, as well as magnesium, vitamin C, and vitamin D are all very helpful. Also, if you have them on hand or can afford them, consider trying sublingual B12, D-ribose, CoQ10, omega-3, NAC, and glutathione. Be sure to check with a trusted health-care professional first.

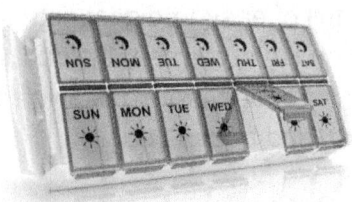

If able to do a little work, take frequent breaks.

For example, you might do some work or an activity for 5 to 15 minutes, then sit down or recline or lie down for 10 to 60 minutes.

Be cautious about going out.

If you leave home (which you're unlikely to be able to do and isn't recommended), avoid driving on your worst days. Walk slowly with whatever aid you need and sit a lot. Or, of course, use a cane, walker, or wheelchair if you need it. If it's sunny, wear sunglasses and a hat with a brim. Also, avoid noise and noisy places.

How to Get a Better Night's Sleep

One of the symptoms of ME/CFS is non-restorative sleep—another reason why we're fatigued during the day. But there's hope. Here are some habits that should make your nighttime sleep more restful, so you'll feel more refreshed in the morning.

Maintain a sleep schedule.

Try to get up and go to bed at roughly the same time every day. This helps regulate your body's internal clock.

Get plenty of natural sunlight during the day,

especially in the morning. This helps regulate your body's internal clock and promotes better sleep at night.

Work at staying calm during the day.

Practicing stress-reduction techniques such as yoga, meditation, or deep breathing during the day can help calm your mind and make it easier to fall asleep.

Try to get some exercise during the day,

preferably outside in the fresh air and daylight—perhaps a short walk, some tai chi, or some yoga. But avoid exercise during the last few hours before bed, to allow your body time to relax.

Avoid napping late in the day.

While short naps can be rejuvenating, avoid napping too close to your bedtime, as it can interfere with your ability to fall asleep at night.

Avoid caffeine at least four hours before bed.

That includes coffee, black or green tea, and chocolate.

Turn off electronics and screens an hour before bed.

The blue light emitted by phones, tablets, computers, and TVs can disrupt your body's production of melatonin.

Don't drink too many liquids before bed.

You don't want to be getting up too many times in the night!

Avoid large meals, heavy foods, or hard-to-digest snacks close to bedtime.

Also, spicy or acidic foods can cause acid reflux and disrupt your sleep.

Avoid sweet snacks before bed,

as the sugar will stimulate your body. Try for a healthier snack such as yogurt with applesauce, a small bowl of light cereal with milk, or crackers with peanut butter and sliced banana.

Create a relaxing bedtime routine,

like reading or listening to an audiobook, doing some gentle yoga, or having a warm bath with low lighting and some Epsom salts.

Once in bed, you may find it soothing to listen to nature sounds or an app designed for relaxation.

Sleep in a dark, quiet room, not too hot or cold.

Maybe invest in some blackout curtains. Running a fan, faced away, helps some people tune out noises. For a better sleep during hot weather, see the chapter on regulating your body temperature.

Wear a sleep mask and earplugs if needed

so you won't be kept awake or awakened by sounds or light.

Move electronic devices that emit blue light

off your bedside table. They can interfere with your body's production of melatonin, a hormone that regulates sleep.

Set your cell to "dark" and "mute."

If you're checking your cellphone before bed or using it to play some mindless games, go to Display, reduce the brightness, and change the light setting to dark.

Open a window for some fresh air, if possible, even just a crack.

If you awaken in the night, talk soothingly to yourself:

"Relax, you're still resting." Or count your breaths, in and out, in and out. Or think about something pleasant.

Avoid looking at the clock.

Constantly checking the time can increase your anxiety and make it harder to fall back to sleep. Turn the clock away from your view.

If, after a while, you still can't sleep, get up for a short time.

Do something quiet and relaxing until you feel sleepy. Maybe walk around a bit in the dim light, read, listen to a soothing audiobook, or work on a jigsaw puzzle or an easy hobby. Keep the lights as low as possible.

As soon as you wake up in the morning, get some light.

Open your curtains or go to a bright room or outside to get some sun or daylight, to help set your circadian rhythm.

These are a lot of sleep hygiene habits to keep in mind, but if you're consistent with them, you should be rewarded with more restful sleep and less daytime fatigue.

Seek professional help.

Of course, if you continue to have difficulty sleeping, it would be a good idea to consult a healthcare professional to rule out sleep apnea or other underlying sleep disorders or medical conditions.

Managing Child-Raising with Limited Energy

Raising children is challenging for healthy, fit people, and for those of us with limited energy, dealing with the needs of our children on top of everything else can often feel overwhelming.

Here are some tips to help you navigate parenting while dealing with your own ME/CFS or other energy-limiting condition.

Prioritize self-care.

Taking care of your own health and wellbeing is critical for providing you enough energy to care for your children. Rest whenever you can, eat mindfully, and hydrate throughout the day.

Talk about it with your kids.

Be honest with your children and communicate your situation in age-appropriate words. This can help them understand why you can't manage certain activities and need to rest often and take breaks.

Set realistic expectations—for yourself and others.

Accept and make it clear to other family members that certain activities and tasks are just too difficult for you to manage without negative repercussions. That way, you can avoid raising their hopes only to disappoint them when you can't do it.

When you need to rest,

show your children your spot (couch, bed, recliner) to rest and recharge, and help them realize the importance of rest for you, so you can do things with them once your energy is (at least somewhat) recharged. When you're in that spot, it's quiet time for them too—time to look at or read books, play educational games on their screens, do puzzles, play quietly with their toys, or lie down themselves.

If your child naps, be sure to nap at the same time. You need it!

Ask for and accept help.

Don't hesitate to ask your spouse or partner, family members, and/or friends for help with managing tasks. Hire a housekeeper or cleaner to come in periodically, if you can afford it. This will save you some energy for giving your children the attention they need.

Delegate age-appropriate tasks to your children.

Train your children from a young age to help clear the table, scrape their plate and put it in the sink, pick up after themselves, put their clothes away, tidy their room, etc. Older children can help with laundry, cleaning, easy cooking, and taking out the trash and recycling. A list on your fridge can remind them without you "nagging" them to do tasks. Rewards for tasks completed would help, too.

Break tasks into small, manageable steps,

both for you and for your children. This should help keep you from feeling overwhelmed and your children from feeling overworked.

Establish a routine.

Predictable routines help all family members accept that everyday household tasks (as well as homework) are a normal part of life.

Make healthy snacks and drinks readily available.

If/when you have your children at home all day, and if you have the energy in the morning (or the night before), put a selection of healthy snacks within their reach. Some suggestions: low-sugar dry cereal like oat o's, whole-grain crackers, cheese, boiled eggs, nuts, baby carrots, celery with peanut butter, apple slices, orange segments, etc. Have water or juice on a low shelf of the refrigerator too.

If you're just too tired to cook a meal, you'll know that your children have had nourishing food that day.

Focus on quality time.

Plan simple games and activities you can do with your children that won't drain your energy. Some mutually enjoyable activities could include reading together, doing crafts like making a friendship bracelet; coloring, drawing and enhancing simple art with colored markers, crayons, or pencil crayons; playing a board game or other game together on a tablet, laptop, or smartphone; doing a jigsaw puzzle on a coffee table or the floor by your sofa; or watching a non-violent, low-key show.

Connect with other parents with limited energy.

Online communities and support groups can provide valuable advice, empathy, and a sense of belonging.

Tips for Working Remotely

Working remotely for an employer or on your own home business is challenging when you have limited energy and reduced physical and cognitive capacity. Here are some tips to help you effectively manage your at-home job while taking care of your health.

Set up a dedicated workspace.

If you have the space, organize a workspace that's away from your relaxation areas. This will help you mentally separate work from rest.

Create an ergonomic setup.

To avoid physical discomfort, strain, or pain, invest in an adjustable office chair with good back support and an ergonomic keyboard and mousepad. Set your monitor low enough to be comfortable to look at without bending your neck back. Also, set up a low stool or some thick books on the floor under your desk to rest your feet on.

Or use a laptop.

If you don't have the room for a separate workspace with a desk, try working on your laptop on a pillow or laptop stand on your bed, recliner, or easy chair. That way, your feet can be raised, and you should be able to work for longer without tiring.

Use assistive tools.

To reduce the physical demands of your work, consider using voice recognition software, text-to-speech programs, or other assistive technologies.

Establish a routine.

To help manage your energy levels and avoid overwhelm, create a daily schedule that includes designated work hours, breaks, and rest periods.

Set realistic goals.

Be pragmatic about what you can accomplish in a day. Overloading yourself with tasks will cause you stress, which can trigger exhaustion. Use a to-do list and prioritize the tasks for the day.

Prioritize tasks.

Identify your most important tasks of the day or week and focus on completing those during your most productive times of the day.

Take frequent breaks.

Regular short breaks can help prevent overexertion and maintain your energy levels. Use a timer or alarm to remind yourself to take breaks.

Rest deliberately and mindfully.

During breaks and rest periods, either rest in darkness with earplugs or try some relaxation techniques such as deep breathing, meditation, listening to nature sounds, or gentle stretching to recharge your energy.

Manage stress.

To minimize the emotional and mental toll of work demands and deadlines, practice stress management techniques, such as meditation, spending time in nature, and listening to or moving to music you love.

Vary your attention and movements.

Change from cognitive effort to physical effort. Get up from the computer and walk around, rotate your shoulders and stretch your arms, go get a snack and beverage, maybe put in a load of laundry or go outside for a while, then go back to work for a while.

Pay attention to your diet and hydration.

Eating nutritious meals and snacks and staying hydrated can help you work more productively.

Know your limits.

Listen to your body and recognize when you need to rest or adjust your schedule. Pushing too hard can lead to setbacks in your health, which could negatively affect your job.

Delegate home tasks.

To help lighten your overall workload and reduce stress, try to delegate some at-home tasks to family members.

Stay connected.

To combat feelings of loneliness and being "out of the loop," make an effort to stay connected with colleagues and friends through texts, phone calls, virtual meetings, or social networks.

Communicate with your employer.

If you feel it's safe to do so, keep your supervisor up to date on your condition and abilities, and discuss potential accommodations that could help you work more effectively. If your supervisor is aware of your limitations, that could help prevent getting last-minute deadlines that could jeopardize your health.

Or choose what to reveal to clients.

If you have your own business and communicate with clients, you may wish to do what I did for years with my freelance book editing business: I didn't discuss my condition or limitations. Rather, I exaggerated a bit the number of other clients I was working with at the same time. Also, if we were actively emailing or texting back and forth and I needed a nap or rest, I just said I'd get back to them later as I had an appointment to go to or errands to run.

If, like so many of us, despite your energy-limiting condition, you can't afford to not work, it's essential to create an optimal work setup, environment, and schedule—with built-in rests—to avoid burnout.

COPING WITH BRAIN FOG AND
THE BLUES

Strategies for Managing Brain Fog

Helpful Techniques for When Your Mind Feels Like Sludge

Be kind to yourself and use positive self-talk.

Frustration will only make your cognitive fuzziness worse. If trying to remember where you put something or how to do a task is making you frustrated, try to calm yourself down with self-affirmations and encouragement. You can tell yourself, "Slow down, I'll get it," "I can do this—I just need to take my time," "Stay calm," or "Keep breathing."

Try to calm your nervous system.

Meditation, breathing exercises, and easy yoga can all help you prevent and manage brain fog. For more ideas, see the chapter, "Calm Your Nervous System."

Stay hydrated and nourished.

- Drink plenty of water all day and take some electrolytes.
- For energy, eat something nutritious that's easy to digest.

Take lots of breaks.

Rest often throughout the day. As your energy picks up, your cognitive abilities will too.

Reduce sensory input and stimulation.

To give your body a break, wear an eye mask and earplugs or noise-canceling headphones whenever you need them. Even more restful for recharging your body battery—go into a quiet, dark room to lie down.

Alert family and friends.

Tell anyone who often calls you that you can't talk today. Or explain that you can talk for only 5 or 10 minutes. If you feel up to texting, mention that you can only do brief texts today.

Simplify activities.

Look for ways to simplify or delegate cognitive tasks. Work for shorter periods of time and take frequent breaks. Plan to do a more difficult task or project another day, or strategize how to simplify it or get out of it. Or you could break it down into smaller tasks and do one of them.

Stay within your cognitive energy envelope.

Straining to do something too difficult for you at that moment will just cause stress and deplete your energy quickly. It could also cause/worsen PEM. Save difficult tasks for when you're feeling mentally sharper.

Take brain breaks.

Spend time each day *not* watching TV, reading, listening to an audiobook, playing games on your (phone or tablet, surfing the web, or catching up on social media. Sitting in nature is always a pleasant alternative if you can do that. Give your brain a rest from time to time!

Memory Helpers for Those "Senior Moments"

Hacks to Help You Remember Things

When you're heading out the door:

- Place keys, wallet or purse, glasses, and sunglasses on a hook, shelf, or cupboard near your door.

- Put anything else you need to take—grocery bags, umbrella, cane, etc.—near the door.

- Put smaller things you want to take in a bag and hang the bag on the doorknob or place it by your outdoor footwear.

- As you're leaving, have a little reminder you repeat to yourself, like, "Phone, keys, wallet."

Reminder aids at home:

- Verbalize.

- Say out loud why you're going to another room or another floor of your house. For example, "I'm looking for scissors."

- Use Post-it notes.

- Stick them on mirrors, by your door, on your desk or table, on the kitchen counter, and wherever you need them.

Use to-do lists.

Prioritize important tasks and deadlines. Write less-important tasks in pencil or on a separate list.

Make note cards for frequent tasks.

I have small note cards, a bit bigger than business cards, in my junk drawer in the kitchen. Each card has a task written on it with marker. Every day, I pull out one or two (or more) to remind me of things I need to do that day. I place them on my stove or kitchen counter, where I can't miss them. These tasks, which might be done twice a week or every three to four weeks, don't fit on the calendar, as they don't have a specific day or time. Some examples: haircut, laundry, run dishwasher, water plants, garbage out, recycling out, wash hair, boil eggs, clean out fridge, defrost freezer.

Put things back in their place.

Try to remember to always return things to their usual spot when you're finished with them, such as marker, tape, scissors, nail clipper, etc., so when you need them again, you can find them quickly, avoiding frustration.

When you come back into your home, be sure to hang your keys back on their hook or wherever they go. That saves frustration next time you go out. Have your wallet or purse in a designated spot too.

Tips for cooking, baking, and using recipes:

- Place a printed recipe in a plastic cover and, with a washable or erasable marker, check off each item as you add it.

- Gather all the ingredients and put them on one area of the counter. As you add each one, move it to another area of the counter. That keeps you from wondering, *Did I add the salt?* and ending up with over-salted muffins or cookies!

Dealing with Fuzzy Brain While Conversing with Others

Participating in a conversation when you're tired and having trouble focusing and expressing yourself can be frustrating and stressful. Here are a few tips to help.

When you can't find the word you're looking for:

- Try to say it in another way by using a synonym or description.

- Use hand gestures and facial expressions.

- Say, "Sorry, I need a minute," or "I need more coffee," or "You know what I mean," or "It's on the tip of my tongue."

Forgot someone's name?

Run through the alphabet in your mind to see which letter it begins with. Also, after being introduced to someone, repeat their name to yourself (or to them) periodically while speaking to them.

Don't be put on the spot.

If someone asks you to do them a favor, give an opinion, or make a decision, and you can't think straight at the moment, just say, "I'll get back to you," or "I need to think about that for a few days."

Be prepared.

Before an appointment, meeting, or Zoom call, create a list of the points you want to make. Have the list in front of you in a brief point form that's easy to skim. Rehearse what you want to say and the words you'll use.

Use Technology to Make Your Life Easier

Techie devices can play a big part in helping you stay organized.

Your Smartphone/ Mobile

These days, who can manage without a smartphone? I'd be lost without mine.

Many of you already use your phones expertly and confidently for communicating in multiple ways, searching for information, watching news, shows, movies, and YouTube, reading e-books, and generally keeping your life and time organized. Others of you might still be discovering ways to use your phone to its full advantage.

If set up properly, your cellphone can be an efficient private secretary, and its size and light weight make it easy to keep with you everywhere.

Here are some of the many ways to use your smartphone to simplify your life and avoid frustration:

Keep in touch. Use it in a variety of ways to communicate with others: for calling, emailing, texting, direct messages, video calls, virtual appointments, and Zoom meetings.

Emergencies: Use it to quickly make an emergency call if needed. Be sure to set up the speed dial function for your emergency contacts.

Take photos to help with memory and eyesight:

- **Take photos of small print** on meds bottles, food labels, or menus, then enlarge them on the Gallery app to read them.

- **Take photos of items in stores and their price**, for comparison shopping.

- **Take photos of things for art/craft ideas**. Carry photos of your rooms in your gallery.

- **Snap a pic of your parking stall number** and area, **a poster** that interests you, **a notice** you'll want to remember later, etc.

- And of course, **photos of family and friends**, as well as **interesting places** you've been.

Keep track of appointments and daily tasks. Use the **Calendar** app to remind yourself of things you need to do and places you need to be. Tell it how long before the event or task it should remind you. You can also set recurring reminders for tasks.

Use the Notes app for all your lists. It's so helpful for various shopping lists, book titles to look for, to-do lists, and other notes. No more leaving paper lists at home!

Use Google to search for information and clarification on various topics on the Internet.

Shop online. Order groceries for pickup or delivery, buy household items from Amazon and other online stores.

Find locations and directions. Use Google Maps to find restaurants, shops, and services nearby, plus open hours, contact info, customer ratings, directions, and how long it will take to get there. So much quicker than the old Yellow Pages!

Scroll social media sites. Facebook, Instagram, Pinterest, TikTok, and other social media sites can be such a lifesaver for people like us who just don't have the energy to socialize a lot in person. You can search for groups of people who share your interests or special needs.

Watch videos on YouTube. There's an amazing variety offered on a huge range of topics.

Connect with other ME/CFS or fibromyalgia groups on Facebook or Instagram. These groups offer much-needed support and networking, and there are lots of them to choose from.

Listen to audiobooks. Listening to an absorbing novel or nonfiction on a topic that interests you can entertain you when you're puttering around, tidying a space, sorting a drawer, or cleaning up the kitchen. Chirp has lots of discounted audiobooks, or, for free loans of audiobooks, try Overdrive, Libby, or Hoopla. Or try Librivox to listen to classics for free.

Read e-books on your Kindle, phone, or tablet.

Get the free Kindle app on your phone as well as the Alexa app and ask Alexa to read your Kindle e-books aloud to you.

Relax and fall asleep easier with calming apps. Apps such as Headspace, Calm, Bearable, and Aura help with relaxation, meditation, and falling asleep.

Play games: There's a huge variety of free games to choose from, including solitaire, jigsaw puzzles, word puzzles, and coloring.

Stream movies and news broadcasts.

Listen to your favorite **radio stations**.

Use the clock to:

- Give you the **time** in your time zone or anywhere around the world.

- Set a wake-up **alarm**.

- Set the **timer** when cooking or baking or to remind yourself to stop working and take a break.

- Use the **stopwatch**.

Find out the **weather** before going out.

Use the handy **calculator** for all your arithmetic needs.

Read Word docs and PDFs. Helpful if you're away from your computer.

Do some writing. Use Notepad or Word to do a bit of writing on your phone.

Use the voice-to-text function (microphone). Easy and convenient for sending text messages, taking notes, and setting reminders.

Use the Record function. Record talks or presentations, an interview, bird songs, notes to yourself, and more. Perfect for recording a visit to your lawyer, doctor, or other health professional.

Connect to your smartwatch. Check how your day is going from data transferred from your smartwatch to your phone. How high is your heart rate? Stress level? How many steps did you take, and how well did you sleep? Monitor your overall body battery fluctuations.

For best results, be sure to use these apps consistently.

If you want these apps to help you remember important appointments and daily tasks, it's essential to actually enter the appointment or birthday in the calendar and add the food item you're almost out of to the grocery list!

Once you make a habit of it, it gets easier and easier, and you won't have the frustration of missing appointments or birthdays or forgetting to buy essentials. Or going to a bookstore or library and being unable to remember which authors or titles you wanted to get.

A Smartwatch (Sports Watch)

Many people with ME/CFS and long COVID depend on their smartwatch to help with pacing and remind them to stop, sit, slow down, and relax, thus preventing PEM.

I find my Garmin Vívoactive really useful. I rely heavily on it to tell me when my heart rate or stress level is too high and when I've taken enough or too many steps. (See the chapter, "Keep Track of Your Heart Rate.")

Garmin's phone app, Connect, also shows me how my "body battery" is doing—if my energy is getting dangerously low and it's time to rest and recharge. It also shows me how I've slept and even notifies me when my stress seems elevated.

As well, I've set it up for specific notifications, so it vibrates when I receive an email, text, message, or reminder from my calendar. It's convenient to be able to actually read short messages, emails, and notes right on my watch.

New smartwatches:

An increasing number of new smartwatches are coming out aimed at seniors, which would work well for people with limited energy and brain fog.

For example, besides time, date, weather, notifications, and more, they indicate:

- daily steps taken
- stress level
- sleep quality
- heart rate
- body battery (fatigue)

and the new ones also indicate:

- blood pressure
- blood oxygen levels
- and more

For more information on the best smartwatches for people with ME, long COVID, or any kind of chronic fatigue, you can google it or join some Facebook groups dedicated to this topic.

> "The Garmin Vivosmart 5 has quickly become a major tool to help me manage my ME/CFS symptoms. When I wake up in the morning, the Body Battery tells me at a glance how much energy I have for the day, which is generally around 37%. It also lets me know which activities are stressful for my body, and which ones aren't. For instance, in the attached image, I can see that working on my computer while lying down charges my body battery, whereas cooking dinner and watching television with my family drains me.

> But the most important thing is that—for the very first time—I have a visual representation of the illness which I can share with my family and doctors. My crippling exhaustion is no longer imaginary or insignificant."

>   - Rae Knightly, author

The white line indicates your energy level (body battery). The high spikes are exertion/stress, and the lower spikes are rest.

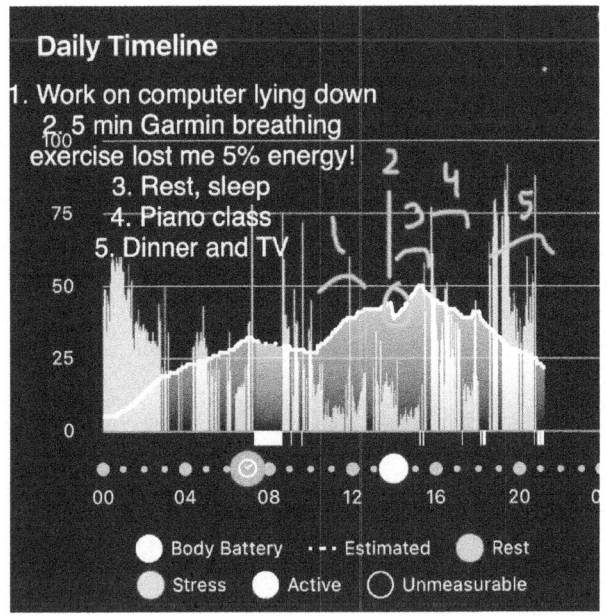

Ask Alexa—or Siri or Bixby

If you don't already have one, I recommend getting an Echo or Echo Dot device or something similar. Or get the Alexa app on your phone. Here's what your Echo or similar device can do for you:

- Play music, answer questions, read the news, check the weather, set alarms, turn lights off and on, control compatible smart home devices, and more.

- Control your music by voice command. Stream songs from Amazon Music, Apple Music, Sirius XM, Spotify, Deezer, and others.

- Read to you from your audiobook from Audible.

- Read aloud to you from e-books on your Kindle e-reader.

- Connect with others. Call almost anyone hands-free. Instantly drop in on other rooms in your home or make an announcement to every room with a compatible Echo device.

- If you can't find your phone, ask Alexa to call you. It works!

"Alexa – Play spa music."

Other Handy Devices

I'm sure many of you already have these as well.

A tablet (iPad):

These are very handy for accessing most of the things your smartphone will do but in a little bigger format and with a bigger screen that's easier to see. Better for reading e-books on your Kindle app, communicating via video calls or Zoom meetings, and watching YouTube videos, news, or movies. You can also get a small separate keyboard to use with it.

A Kindle or other e-reader:

You can adjust the style and size of the font, as well as the lighting to read in the dark, low light, or bright light. You can highlight text, bookmark sections, make notes to yourself, and, if you don't have the focus to read, ask Alexa to read a book aloud to you.

Can't afford a Kindle?

> Download the **free Kindle app** to your phone, tablet, laptop, or PC.

Habits & Attitudes for Staying Positive

Staying positive while dealing with a chronic illness can be challenging, but it's important for your overall well-being to find ways to do so. Here are some strategies to help you maintain a positive outlook.

Practice self-compassion.

Be kind and patient with yourself. Treat yourself with the same compassion that you would show a friend in a similar situation.

Practice acceptance.

Accepting your condition doesn't mean giving up, but, instead of fighting against it or trying to deny it, acknowledging your situation and working on ways to deal with it can reduce your frustration and stress.

Educate yourself on your condition.

Learn as much as you can about your condition from reliable sources. Understanding it better can help you make informed decisions about your treatment and self-care.

Set realistic goals.

Goals give us something to look forward to and strive for. Be sure your goals are not unrealistic. To avoid frustration and discouragement, they need to be achievable and flexible. As with housework, break larger goals into smaller, manageable steps.

Stay connected with others.

Keep up communications with friends and family, even if it's just the occasional text, phone call, or in-person visit. And for emotional support and a feeling of belonging, join some support groups on Facebook and Instagram.

Focus on the positive.

Every day, try to think about some of the positive aspects of your life, the things you can still enjoy and appreciate. When talking with close friends or family, don't dwell on the limitations of your current lifestyle; instead, find something pleasant to talk about and ask them about their lives.

Make time for enjoyable activities.

Engaging in hobbies and easy, manageable activities you enjoy can boost your mood. See the chapter on pastimes and hobbies.

Limit negative input.

Avoid watching or listening to a lot of negative or depressing news reports. Also, avoid "toxic" people or any situations that could leave you angry, frustrated, or depressed. Surround yourself with positivity as much as possible.

Stay engaged with positive aspects of the world.

On TV, YouTube, and streaming on your laptop, watch travel videos and virtual tours of special places, nature shows, food and cooking shows, competitions, world-class performances, sports events, and special cultural events to stay connected with the greater world.

Help others.

Engaging in acts of kindness, even from home, can create a sense of purpose and positivity. Just listening to a family member or friend who's having a stressful time can make a huge difference to them. Brainstorm ways to volunteer virtually on your good days. Maybe help an immigrant with their spoken English (or another language) or help someone learn to knit, crochet, or paint via Zoom.

Celebrate small wins.

Give yourself a pat on the back for every little goal you reach or job you achieve, no matter how small. Resist comparing yourself to what your healthy peers are able to do.

Look for humor around you.

A sense of humor and laughing can lighten your mood and brighten your day. Watch a humorous television show or movie, read or listen to a funny book, follow a comedian or satirist on social media.

Try creative hobbies.

Learn an easy musical instrument, dabble in doodling, drawing, or painting, experiment with collage or photography, learn to crochet or knit, write poetry or a short story, or explore other ways to be creative.

Keep learning.

When you feel up to it, keep your mind active with time-flexible online courses, virtual museum tours, educational videos, or by reading or listening to books you've been meaning to get to. That will give you a sense of connection and accomplishment.

Hug it out!

While I wouldn't recommend hugging just anyone—at least not without their consent—you can absolutely start a hugging habit with family, a partner/spouse, and friends! If you're not sure, just ask. You can also be a super-spreader of virtual hugs in texts, emails, and other online networks. For pet parents, when other humans aren't nearby, give your fur baby a cuddle.

Nurture some plants.

Whether it's houseplants or something in your yard, connecting with nature will help ground you and elevate your mood.

Create a beautiful corner or spot in your home.

Clear off a space and arrange some things you love in a pleasing arrangement there. Maybe a vase or small sculpture, a plant or some flowers, some special rocks or seashells, or something you've created yourself.

Morning Lift

I wake up
limbs heavy
joints stiff
head aching
I lie there
wonder if getting up
is even worth it

But then
a movement outside my window
catches my eye
Goldfinch flies by
stops at the feeder for a fill
Nuthatch joins him
digging for peanuts
and Chickadee
cracks black oil sunflower seeds
in his precise little beak

Each flutter of wing
each bob and hop
reaches me and lifts
invisible pull
until I'm risen
These birds
my support network

~ Michele Rule

121

Tips for Calming Your Mind and Nervous System

Staying as calm as possible is essential to avoid further stressing your already damaged, struggling mitochondria and to allow your body to repair itself and produce more energy.

Stress, anxiety, and tension will zap your energy faster than anything else.

Perhaps you've got something on your mind or are stressed about something. Or maybe you've been running on adrenaline and now need desperately to rest, but you're "tired but wired" and can't seem to relax enough to nap or sleep.

Here are some effective techniques for dealing with stress, anxiety, fear, and worry and for calming a hyperactive brain and body.

How To Avoid Getting Too Anxious or Tense

Limit stimulants.

Reduce or eliminate the consumption of caffeine, nicotine, sugar, and other stimulants. These substances can exacerbate racing thoughts and anxiety.

Avoid or limit alcohol.

Alcohol depletes energy and can cause depression.

Establish a routine.

Having a daily routine can provide structure and reduce the sense of chaos in your mind. Make sure to include time for relaxation and self-care in your schedule.

Make a to-do list.

Write a list of tasks you feel you need to get done, in order of priority. This eliminates the need to try to remember them. And crossing them off the list as you do them provides a sense of accomplishment.

Better yet, make a "done" list.

List everything you got accomplished in a day, down to the smallest tasks. Include things like drank water, cleaned the sink, wiped the counter, tidied my workspace, texted a friend, etc.

Limit multitasking.

Try to focus on one task at a time instead of juggling multiple tasks simultaneously. This can help reduce mental clutter.

Limit news consumption.

Constant exposure to negative news can contribute to an overactive mind. Consider setting specific times for checking the news and avoid excessive exposure.

Practice gratitude.

Regularly remind yourself of the positive aspects of your life. Hopefully you have a home and enough food to eat, for example, or a hobby you enjoy. Gratitude can shift your focus away from negative thoughts.

Find joy in small things in your life.

Savor the taste of your favorite beverage or food, the coziness of your bathrobe or favorite socks or slippers, the play of light and shadows out your window, a sunrise or sunset, cloud patterns, the sound of the rain, a favorite tune, a cute baby or pet, a funny joke, enjoying a favorite hobby or pastime.

Try journaling.

If it's more of a general busyness and anxiety, consider writing down your thoughts and feelings in a journal. This can help you gain clarity and release pent-up emotions.

Or track your moods with a **thought map**. In a circle in the middle of a piece of paper, name your mood. Around it, make more circles and write in each a specific related to that mood.

Or try the **apps** Moodnotes or What's Up? a mental health app.

Consciously Relax Your Muscles.

Try progressive muscle relaxation.

Tense and then release each muscle group in your body, starting from your toes and working your way up to your head. This can help relieve physical tension associated with an anxious or overactive mind.

Sink into the bed.

Lie on your bed or another comfortable surface and consciously encourage your body to feel heavier and sink into the bed. Start with your shoulders, then continue with your arms and hands, and so on, consciously relaxing each part of your body and feeling yourself sinking lower.

Scrunch and relax.

On your bed, sofa, or a rug or yoga mat, bring your knees up and hug yourself tightly, tightening all your muscles, for 10–30 seconds. Then lie back and relax all your muscles for 10–30 seconds. Repeat a few times. You might find it easier to do this from a propped-up position, rather than lying flat.

Relax in a hot or warm bath.

Add some Epsom salts and use low lighting or candlelight. Try to clear your mind and just feel your muscles relaxing and the tension leaving your body. (In hot weather, make it a cool bath.)

Gently move your body.

Any regular physical activity you are able to do without causing PEM can help burn off excess energy and improve your mood. Even a short walk or some gentle stretching can be beneficial.

Or move to some music. Dance, if you can manage it, or just move slowly to music with your feet stationary.

Or just do some easy, relaxed stretches on your bed, rug, or yoga mat.

Try Guided Relaxation Techniques.

Practice mindfulness meditation.

Mindfulness meditation involves paying attention to the present moment without judgment. It can help you become more aware of your thoughts and feelings and reduce racing thoughts. Start with short sessions and gradually increase the duration as you become more comfortable.

If you're new to meditation, there are some highly rated apps to help you, such as Headspace, Calm, Insight Timer, and Aura. Or you can check YouTube for videos or listen to audiobooks that take you through guided meditation.

Learn/practice deep breathing techniques.

To learn breathing techniques that work for you, search on Google or YouTube, or try the app Breathwrk.

Learn or practice yoga, tai chi, qigong, or Pilates.

Try yin yoga or yoga nidra to help soothe the nervous system and relax excess mental energy so that you can sleep better, longer, and deeper. Or follow a YouTube video on qigong, seated tai chi, or chair yoga.

Relax Your Mind and Calm Your Emotions.

How To Calm an Overactive Mind

Do you find that sometimes your mind just won't shut up? Especially at busy or stressful times or when planning for an outing, trip, event, or company. You're trying to relax, but your brain is still going over all the details of things you need to do.

Here are some effective strategies and techniques for calming your mind as well as your body.

Practice deep breathing.

Deep, slow breathing can help calm your nervous system and reduce anxiety.

Try the **4-7-8 breathing technique**: Inhale for a count of 4, hold for 7 counts, and exhale for 8 counts. Repeat this several times.

Or try **square breathing** or box breathing:

- Begin by slowly exhaling all of your air out.
- Then, gently inhale through your nose to a slow count of 4.
- Hold at the top of the breath for a count of 4.
- Then gently exhale through your mouth for a count of 4.
- At the bottom of the breath, pause and hold for the count of 4.

Visualize a relaxing place.

Imagine yourself relaxing in a favorite nature setting and focus on the details. Try to use all five senses to transport yourself to that ideal spot. What do you see, hear, smell, feel? Maybe even taste?

Listen to soothing sounds.

Nature sounds, instrumental music, or slow, familiar songs are calming and uplifting, either during the day or when trying to relax

126

enough to sleep. **Listen to calming apps** on your phone or other device; for example, "Nature Sounds Relax and Sleep."

Go out and spend time in nature.

Trees are grounding, and a running stream is so soothing. Listen to the wind, water, birds, and other nature sounds. If your mobility is limited, you may need to drive close to a nature trail and then use your cane, walker, wheelchair, or mobility scooter. Or sit outside in your yard or in a park or treed area near your home.

Ground yourself. Consider trying some of the grounding exercises on LivingWell.org.

Sing or hum a familiar tune.

Use reassuring self-talk or mantras, such as:

It'll be all right. You can do this. There's no rush.

Everything doesn't have to be perfect. Take it slow.

You can manage this. You're safe.

Work on an easy craft.

For lots of suggestions for relaxing activities, see the next chapter, "70 Easy Hobbies & Pastimes."

Listen to an audiobook or read an engrossing novel.

Watch TV: Watch a movie, show, or series you enjoy that will take your mind off your worries.

Watch a YouTube video on a subject that interests you—home renos, travel, gardening, painting, flower arranging, cooking, crafts, etc.

Listen to a podcast on a topic that interests you.

Play simple games or do easy activities on your phone or tablet, such as Colorfy for coloring or the Antistress Anxiety Relief Game.

Consider trying calming teas or supplements:

Drink relaxing herbal teas, such as chamomile or various relaxing herbal blends.

Take herbal or vitamin supplements, such as maca or ashwagandha (they also come in chewable tablets) or anti-stress herbal/vitamin blends. **Calcium and magnesium** will also help calm your system.

Bottom line:

Calming a hyperactive body or busy, anxious mind can take time and practice, so be patient with yourself. Experiment with different techniques to find which ones work best for you.

If your overactive mind or hyperactive nervous system are causing significant distress or interfering with your daily life, consider talking to a mental health professional.

70 Easy Hobbies & Pastimes

Even though chronic fatigue can be challenging to manage, there are still many hobbies and pastimes that those of us with low energy can manage and enjoy. Working on arts and crafts is a great way to pick up your mood and express your creativity.

Even when working on hobbies, it's essential to pace yourself and listen to your body, so you don't overexert. Maybe set a timer to remind you to take a break before getting overtired.

Here's an extended list of over 70 relatively easy, enjoyable hobbies and pastimes to choose from:

VISUAL ARTS

Drawing: Start with pencils of varying softness and an eraser. As your confidence builds, try using charcoal, markers, chalk pastels, paint pens, oil pastels, etc.

Painting: New to painting? Check out YouTube for excellent how-to videos and inspiration. Experiment with various media and techniques for different effects.

Painting rocks for your yard, balcony, or elsewhere. Using permanent paint pens is the easiest way. Ask friends or family to collect some nice round ones with a flat surface for you to paint on, and then they or you can leave the painted ones alongside walking trails.

Multi-media artistic creations on canvas or wood. Arrange, then glue on whatever found objects you like— fabric, yarn, string, sticks, leaves, dried flowers, paper, cardboard, buttons, etc.

Wall fabric art: Experiment with different textures, colors, and designs.

129

Coloring in an adult coloring book. For a more satisfying result, use pencil crayons instead of markers, so you can erase and lighten. Plus, you can experiment with shading techniques for more satisfying results.

Painting by numbers: No creative ability or artistic talent needed. Just choose a picture you like. All the decision-making is done for you.

Painting with water: The easiest! Buy "coloring" books that have a scene painted with invisible paint, which you activate by painting on water to bring the image to life.

CRAFTS USING PAPER

Making greeting cards, bookmarks, etc. Create original, personalized gifts for others.

Origami: Craft intricate paper figures.

Quilling: Create art from paper strips.

Collage: Cut pictures from magazines and rearrange, or make a multi-media collage creation.

Scrapbooking: Create a pleasing visual journal of your memories, using favorite photos and other enhancements.

CRAFTS USING FABRIC, YARN, OR THREAD

Sewing: by machine or by hand. Create easy outfits or accessories. Alter or embellish your clothes to make them more attractive or fit better.

Slow sewing: Gaining popularity. Lots of videos on YouTube.

Special sewing projects: Make doll clothes, dolls, or stuffed animals.

Knitting or crocheting: Make decorative items or a throw; baby or doll clothes; or cozy socks, mittens, caps, etc. for yourself or family, friends, or homeless shelters.

Quilting: Try smaller projects, such as a table runner or centerpiece, a bag, or a cushion.

Cross stitch, embroidery: Create wall or table art or decorate napkins, cushions, bags, and more.

Rug hooking, punch needle projects: Can be a little more strenuous on the hands.

Weaving: Start with a small project to build confidence and avoid overtiring.

Felting: Produce a new fabric by combining and compressing loose fibers, wool, or hair.

Macrame: Explore creating with cord—wall hangings, holders for hanging plants, bags, etc.

OTHER CRAFTS

Beadwork: bracelet beading, other jewelry making (earrings are easy)

Diamond painting (bead art): Like paint by number, but you place colored beads on a sticky surface with an image and symbols for different colors.

Miniatures: Try assembling and arranging doll houses or miniature shops or rooms.

Wood carving: Search "wood carving ideas for beginners."

Woodworking: Make a bird house, a box, or a small stool, for example.

Furniture refinishing: Lots of possibilities, but more strenuous, so only attempt if/when able.

OTHER ENJOYABLE PASTIMES

Reading: Escape with a good paperback novel or e-book. Explore different genres and authors. Some people with ME/CFS, long COVID, or other energy-limiting conditions find it less taxing to read a familiar book they've enjoyed in the past or a book written for a young readership (middle-grade or young adult).

Digital scrapbooking: Use your computer, your photos (digital or scanned), and graphics software to create beautiful books showcasing memorable moments.

Indoor gardening: Care for low-maintenance houseplants or succulents.

Collecting: Coins, stamps, or postcards, for instance.

Photography: Capture special moments and images around you. Then you could create a digital scrapbook.

Baking: Try simple recipes with manageable steps.

Cooking: Experiment with easy recipes.

Playing an easy musical instrument. Some light, easy ones to try:

- Kalimba thumb piano
- Small steel tongue drum
- Castanets
- Recorder
- Harmonica

Lego building: Construct structures, working at your own pace and energy level. To start with the easiest ones, get children's ones and go by the age range suggested.

Model airplanes, vehicles, ships, etc. Lots of kits available.

LISTENING & VIEWING

Listening to audiobooks on Audible, Chirp (lots of excellent discounted titles), Spotify, or free from the library with the Libby app. You can change the speed of the narration to slow it down if you need to. And it's really easy to back it up a bit to replay. Or, when listening at bedtime, set a time for it to stop automatically.

Listening to music: Explore new genres or create playlists.

Listening to podcasts on topics that interest you.

Watching YouTube videos. Some suggestions: travel videos; how-to videos on hobbies, crafts, and home décor; easy yoga, chair yoga, and chair tai chi.

Watching short videos, reels, and clips of interest on Facebook, Instagram, TikTok, or other social media.

Watching documentaries: Learn about various topics.

Watching classic movies: Catch up on timeless films.

Virtual tours: Explore museums and landmarks online.

Watching nature shows: Learn about the natural world.

GAMES & PUZZLES

Jigsaw puzzles: There's a huge variety available. I prefer 500 pieces or less—they're easier, and they usually take up less space.

Puzzle books: Sudoku, word searches, crossword puzzles, and more. Choose relatively easy ones that will still challenge your mind without overexerting.

Board games: Enjoy low-energy games with friends or family.

Playing video games. So many different ones available.

Playing games on your tablet or phone: Solitaire, puzzles, coloring, and so many more.

EXERCISING YOUR MIND

Online courses: Learn something new from the comfort of your home.

Learning a new language: Use language learning apps or online courses.

Writing: Start a journal, blog, or write short stories or poetry.

Pen pal writing: Connect with people in other countries through letters.

Social networking: Facebook, Instagram, Pinterest, TikTok, and others.

OUTDOOR ACTIVITIES

Birdwatching and bird feeding: Observe and feed local birds from your window, balcony, deck, or yard.

Geocaching: Outdoor treasure hunting with minimal physical exertion.

Stargazing: Observe the night sky with a telescope or binoculars.

Gardening: Create a small, manageable garden. Enlist some help to make it low maintenance, with raised beds, etc.

Enjoying nature:

- Lie under a tree and look up.

- Sit beside a brook, stream, or river and breathe deeply. What do you see, hear, smell, touch?

- Go to a park and place your painted rocks alongside a nature trail.

Remember that hobbies can be tiring too. When choosing hobbies and pastimes, be sure to adapt the activities to your own energy levels. Take your time and enjoy the process.

Prioritize self-care, listen to your body's needs, and set time limits for rest.

Enjoy!

Some Tips for Beating the Blues

Feeling down or experiencing the "blues" from time to time is a common part of life for everyone, but more so for those of us whose activities are restricted due to low energy.

Here are some general tips that I hope will help you beat the blues and improve your mood.

Prioritize self-care.

Take time for self-care activities like relaxing in a warm bath, reading or listening to a good book, listening to music you love, or working on a hobby you enjoy.

Look for joy in small things.

Savor the pleasant sensation (taste, sound, look, smell, feel) from your tea or coffee, a favorite snack, some chocolate, birds singing, leaves fluttering in the breeze, a favorite tune, interesting shadows created by the light, a funny meme on social media, the feel of a cozy sweater or a smooth surface, or whatever picks you up a little.

Practice gratitude.

Reflect on the things or people you're grateful for, even small ones. Write down at least one thing you're grateful for each day in a journal. Maybe it's your cozy bed, the tree outside your window, or a family member or friend who understands. Reread it when you're "down."

Spend time in nature.

Nature has a calming effect on the mind. Go for a walk in a nature park or along a woodsy trail to do some "forest bathing," or just sit outside and tune in to the sights, sounds, and smells of nature around you.

Engage in creative activities.

Sketching, painting, knitting, crocheting, working on a craft, playing an easy musical instrument, writing some poetry or a short story or memoir, or exploring other creative outlets can be therapeutic and improve your mood.

Set small goals.

Accomplishing even small tasks and checking them off your list can boost your self-esteem and provide a sense of purpose and accomplishment.

Say "no" to negativity.

Avoid "toxic" people and reduce exposure to negative news or social media that might be contributing to your blues.

Get moving.

Physical activity releases endorphins, which are natural mood lifters. If you are able, go for a short walk, dance or sway to some music, do some chair yoga or seated tai chi, or try another type of exercise you know you can manage without PEM.

Reach out to a friend or loved one.

Talking to someone you trust can provide emotional support and help you feel less alone.

Get enough sleep.

Lack of sleep can exacerbate negative emotions. Work on your sleep hygiene to help give your mood a fighting chance.

Limit alcohol and substance use.

These substances can exaggerate feelings of sadness and depression.

Practice mindful eating.

Nutrient-rich foods can give you more energy and positively impact your mood.

Avoid excessive sugar and caffeine, which can give you a false "high" and lead to crashes.

Seek professional help.

If your blues persist or worsen to the point that persistent negative feelings are interfering with your daily life, consider talking to a therapist or counselor who can provide guidance and support. Seeking help when needed is a sign of strength, not weakness.

A few more specific suggestions:

Clean out your junk drawer.

Take out your junk drawer, utensils drawer, underwear/sock drawer, sewing kit, or toolbox, put it on your kitchen table or coffee table, take all the stuff out, and put back what you need, rearranging it. Discard what you don't use. That should give you a sense of satisfaction without a huge amount of effort.

Update your wardrobe.

Buy some very comfortable but flattering at-home clothes in colors that brighten your day—comfortable loungewear or, for the women, a few comfy dresses with pockets, a yoga outfit with pockets, or new pajamas or a nightie. Also, warm socks, slippers, or a cozy bathrobe.

Refresh your living space.

Here are a few easy, low-cost ideas for making your home more attractive, which will help pick up your spirits.

- Get a few brighter hand towels or dish towels to add a spark of color.
- Replace your shower curtain, bathmat, and/or bathroom accessories with a new color scheme.
- Buy new couch cushions or sew new covers for the ones you have.
- Make or buy some new wall art.
- Buy or find a nice, easy-care potted plant.

Slowly declutter your home.

Having fewer things will make your life easier and help you stay organized, easily find what you you're looking for, and stay calm.

See the next chapter on how mess and clutter can be detrimental to our mental and physical health.

For advice on making decluttering less onerous and more manageable, go to the chapter "Decluttering Tips."

Reduce Mess to Reduce Stress

Do you have too much stuff? Are your closets bulging with clothes that no longer fit or appeal to you? Is your desk or kitchen table piled with papers and other items that need to be dealt with? Do you have trouble finding things when you need them? You're definitely not alone!

Many or most of us are too tired to keep a perfect, tidy home. I certainly am, and I prefer to spend my limited energy on other things besides cleaning, tidying, and decluttering.

Unfortunately, the clutter and mess that can build up can have a negative effect on our overall well-being. My research has found a definite connection between clutter and health, which increases my determination to gradually declutter and tidy my own home.

Here are some ways that a messy and cluttered home can have detrimental effects on our mental and physical health.

Mess equals stress

Just looking at clutter can create a sense of chaos, causing mild anxiety and making it difficult to relax.

When everything is in its place, you can quickly grab your cell phone, glasses, keys, tape, scissors, nail clippers, or whatever you need and get on with your day, instead of wasting time and getting frustrated looking for them.

Scattered attention, memory issues, and reduced motivation and productivity

Your brain is wired to be able to keep track of only a few details at once, so it can get overloaded when there's too much around you that needs to be dealt with, leading to forgetfulness and confusion.

A messy, cluttered environment can sap your motivation and energy, making it harder to tackle daily tasks. Too much stuff around you can also hinder your ability to focus and concentrate, making it harder to get work done efficiently. It can be especially tough for people with ADHD (attention deficit hyperactivity disorder).

Allergies and respiratory issues

It's hard to dust or clean those cluttered surfaces. If you're allergic to dust mites or pet dander, decluttering will make it easier to dust and vacuum, which should reduce sneezing, coughing, sore throat, and itchy eyes.

CHAOS – Can't Have Anyone Over Syndrome

I know all about this one. When my clutter and mess are at a high level, I don't invite anyone over, which can exacerbate feelings of isolation and loneliness. Clutter can also lead to arguments and conflicts with family members or roommates, straining relationships. At its worst, living in a cluttered space can lead to feelings of guilt, shame, and overwhelm, negatively impacting your mental well-being.

Tripping Hazards

Living with lots of clutter puts you at risk of getting injured. When your floor is covered with boxes and other stuff, or even too much furniture, it's that much easier to trip and fall.

Increased Fire Hazards

If you've got too much paper, cardboard, and other flammable items hanging around, your home can be a fire hazard, both with more items to catch fire and also more obstacles in the way of getting out quickly.

Poor Sleep

A messy bedroom can make you feel subliminally unsettled, so it might be harder to calm yourself and fall asleep.

Inversely, if you're sleep-deprived, you might be more likely to make questionable decisions, including ones that involve getting more stuff you really don't need.

Bottom line: If you tidy your place, you'll feel better.

When I'm busy or tired, I put off cleaning up the kitchen or putting things away. I try to just ignore the mess. But when I do tidy up a space, like my kitchen counter, table, or office, I feel so much better! I feel calmer, with a satisfied feeling that I've accomplished something, even if it's just an improvement of one corner of my home.

Regular cleaning, organizing, and simplifying of your home environment can contribute to improved mental and physical health, so it's a good goal to try to tackle a bit each day that you feel up to it.

And remember:

Slow progress is still progress!

For guidelines to make the process easier, see the chapter, "Decluttering Tips."

NUTRITION, DIGESTION, AND RECIPES

Nutrition for Energy

"You are what you eat." – Unknown.

Because your energy is limited, it's tempting to just grab some fast food, but your body will thank you if you pause a minute and think about what you're choosing to eat. That way, your food choices will help improve your health rather than making it worse.

Numerous health professionals have discovered a strong relationship between disease and a lack of good nutrition. Conversely, a mindful, high-quality diet can help improve your overall health and give you a better chance of gaining more energy.

Healthy Eating Habits in a Nutshell

Dietary Guidelines for Americans, 2020–2025, suggests that we focus on nutrient-dense foods and beverages that provide vitamins, minerals, and other nutrients and have no or little added sugars, saturated fat, and sodium.

They recommend:

- **Vegetables** of all types and colors, including, for protein, legumes such as beans, peas, and lentils

- **Fruits**, especially whole fruit (fresh or frozen is better than canned or packaged)

- **Grains**, at least half of which are whole grain

- **Dairy**, including milk, yogurt, and cheese, and/or lactose-free versions

- **Protein foods**, including lean meats, poultry, and eggs; seafood; beans, peas, and lentils; and nuts, seeds, and soy products

- **Oils**, including vegetable oils and oils in food, such as seafood and nuts

And we also need to:

"Limit foods and beverages higher in added sugars, saturated fat, and sodium, and limit alcoholic beverages."

Canada's Food Guide says our daily diets should be 50% vegetables and fruit, 25% protein sources, and 25% whole grains. Limit zero foods (junk food).

According to the Food Guide, **our dinner plate should be one-half vegetables**; **one-quarter protein**, such as fish, meat, poultry, seafood, beans, lentils, and tofu; and **one-quarter whole-grain foods**, such as brown rice, wild rice, quinoa, whole-grain pasta, and whole-grain bread. Then have fruit for dessert.

The Canadian food guide also says:

- Make water your drink of choice.

- Read food labels, looking for too much sugar, sodium, or chemicals.

- Limit foods high in sodium, sugars, or saturated fat.

- Limit highly processed foods.

- Be aware of the subtle pressures of food marketing.

Tips for a Nutritious, Energy-Producing Diet

Eat real, whole foods, and limit processed, packaged foods.

Try to shop mainly from the perimeter of the supermarket, where you'll find fresh fruits and vegetables, eggs, dairy, fish, and meats. Also, go to the freezer section to stock up on frozen vegetables and fruit. This option is actually healthier than keeping old vegetables in your fridge, as produce is usually fast-frozen at its peak. And of course, it keeps longer in your freezer. Also, check out baking supplies and the bulk foods section and look for nuts, seeds, dried beans, and whole grains.

Processing largely strips away food's essential nutrients. So when you eat highly processed food in packages, boxes, or cans, you get mainly starches, sugars, additives, and empty calories.

That's why it's best to create your meals and snacks from real ingredients. When you do choose packaged food, check the label for ingredients you recognize as actual food rather than chemicals.

Prioritize fruits and vegetables.

Make half your daily food intake vegetables and fruit. Try to eat a rainbow of colors.

Fresh vegetables and fruits contain important anti-inflammatory compounds that reduce risk for chronic diseases. Try to eat foods listed in the Superfoods section below every day.

Have some fruit for dessert, add berries to yogurt or cereal, and add dark leafy greens and berries or other fruit to smoothies. For snacks, consider a banana, carrot sticks, celery sticks, apple slices, and orange segments. See the list of healthy snack suggestions below.

Eat whole grains, not refined.

Refined white flour has been linked to chronic inflammation, which is implicated in a wide range of diseases, including diabetes and

146

arthritis, according to healthygreensavvy.com and other reliable sources.

Also, eating whole grains will leave you feeling fuller, so you'll likely eat less. Soaking and/or sprouting whole grains makes them even more nutritious. Look for bread, muffins, and other baked goods made from sprouted grains.

Avoid chemicals.

Eat real, whole foods. When buying packaged or canned, read labels carefully. Banish sugary cereals, diet sodas, and artificially flavored and colored drinks from your cupboards.

Cut way back on sugar.

Sugar might give you a quick burst of energy, but, like the effects of caffeine, it's not real energy, so it can make you expend energy you don't really have, resulting in a deficit or low, leaving you feeling worse than before you had the sugar.

If you reduce your sugar intake gradually and start comparing the sugar content of drinks and foods, it won't be long before you'll prefer the lower-sugar versions.

Save sweet treats for after a meal, when your stomach is already full, rather than consuming them on an empty stomach.

Also, read and compare the sugar content in soups, pasta sauces, salad dressings, cookies, canned fruit, granola bars, sweetened yogurt, cookies, and chocolate bars.

Watch for all the different types of added sugar, including corn syrup, cane syrup, brown rice syrup, fructose, dextrose, maltose, and sucrose. They're all sugar.

A few everyday ways to reduce your sugar intake:

- Plain yogurt tastes great with berries, fruit, and/or granola. Or you could combine yogurt and unsweetened applesauce, with maybe a little maple syrup. Add chia seeds to that and let it sit for a few hours or overnight for a delicious chia pudding.

- Make your own granola or muesli with no added sugar (or at least reduced honey or other sweetener).

- When baking, use half the sugar suggested or replace all or most of it with chopped dates, applesauce, or mashed banana.

Eat more protein.

Have a high-protein breakfast and protein at each snack and meal. Try to eat some protein every 2 to 3 hours. Protein gives you more sustained stamina, rather than the quicker burst of energy and the subsequent crash that you get from sugar and caffeine.

Choose lean, healthy protein.

Good sources of protein include eggs, fish, beans, and lentils. For meat, choose grain-fed beef (in moderation) and chicken, preferably organic.

Follow the Mediterranean diet.

According to the Mayo Clinic, "Plant-based foods, such as whole grains, vegetables, legumes, fruits, nuts, seeds, herbs and spices, are the foundation of the [Mediterranean] diet. Olive oil is the primary source of added fat. Fish, seafood, dairy and poultry are included in moderation. Red meat and sweets are eaten only occasionally."

Be sure to have some healthy fats and oils every day.

Salmon, avocados, nuts, nut butters, olive oil, coconut oil, and avocado oil are all sources of healthy fats, which are essential for good health.

Avoid eating large, heavy meals.

Digesting food takes a lot of precious energy, leaving you extra tired. Besides avoiding hard-to-digest foods, it's best to eat three light meals a day, plus two or three nutritious snacks.

Stay hydrated.

This advice can't be overemphasized, which is why it's repeated several times in this book. Dehydration will exacerbate your fatigue because many body processes require water.

Have some electrolytes every day.

A few recommended electrolytes are Liquid IV, ViDrate sachets, and DripDrop. Coconut water works well, too. Or make your own by adding 1-2 tsp lemon juice, 1 tsp honey, and a pinch of salt to a glass or cup of water.

Some Easy, High-Protein Snacks

- A handful of almonds, cashews, walnuts, peanuts, pistachios, or mixed nuts (toasted or roasted for easier digestion)

- Roasted pumpkin seeds or sunflower seeds

- Trail mix

- Protein bar

- Healthy cookies

- Cheese with crackers or apple slices

- Celery with peanut butter, other nut butters, or hummus

- Hard-boiled egg on a rice thin

- Hummus with crackers or baby carrots

- Canned salmon or tuna on crackers

- Nut butter on crackers or toast

- Greek yogurt with berries and/or granola

- Cottage cheese and fruit cocktail, berries, or other fruit

- No-bake energy bites (see recipe)

- Jerky

- Nut butter on apple slices or celery sticks

- Dark chocolate with walnuts, hazelnuts, or almonds

- Smoothies with protein powder

- Toast spread with peanut butter or other nut butter. Top with currants, sliced banana, or sliced apple.

Protein Content of Various Milks

Cow's milk is a good source of calcium and protein, with 8 g of protein per cup.

But many of us are intolerant or sensitive to dairy – not only the lactose, but also the two milk proteins, casein and whey. Here are some alternatives to dairy milk, with the protein content of each per cup:

Protein content of various milks, per 8 fluid ounces, from Healthline.com and wellandgood.com:

1. Soy milk: 7-8 g

2. Pea milk: 7-8 g

3. Cashew milk: 4 g

4. Oat milk: 3-4 g

5. Hemp milk: 3 g

6. Flaxseed milk: 3 g

7. Almond milk: 2 g

8. Rice milk: 0 g

9. Coconut milk: 0 g

Note: Unless they're enriched with calcium and vitamin D, none of the dairy milk alternatives provide as much of those nutrients as dairy milk does.

Good news: Recently I discovered in my supermarket a blend of **almond and cashew milk** with added pea protein that has **8 g of protein**. It's enriched with vitamins and minerals as well. Since it's also delicious, this has become my go-to choice of milks.

Superfoods

"Superfoods" is a term used in the health and wellness industry to describe foods that are exceptionally rich in nutrients and are believed to have the potential to improve overall health, boost energy, and prevent or manage various diseases.

Superfoods are foods packed with nutrients like vitamins, minerals, and antioxidants, which fight free radicals that cause cellular damage.

You'll find about 50 superfoods listed online, with new ones being added every year. The list below is gleaned from several websites and based on everyday, easy-to-find, non-exotic foods.

Try to eat several foods from this list every day for increased energy and maximum health benefits:

Dark leafy greens: Spinach, kale, Swiss chard, collard greens, turnip greens, and mixed greens are high in vitamins, minerals, and fiber.

Berries: Blueberries, raspberries, black raspberries, cranberries, strawberries, pomegranates, goji berries, and other berries are rich in antioxidants and vitamins.

Eggs: Eggs are a source of complete, high-quality protein; are rich in many other vitamins and minerals; and contain antioxidants that are known to protect vision and eye health.

Salmon: Salmon is a highly nutritious fish packed with healthy omega-3 fatty acids, protein, B vitamins, and minerals.

Legumes: Beans, lentils, peas, and peanuts are a rich source of B vitamins, various minerals, protein, and much-needed fiber.

Olive oil: An essential part of the Mediterranean diet, olive oil contains antioxidants such as vitamins E and K, which can protect against cellular damage from oxidative stress.

Extra-virgin olive oil, which is green, is more beneficial than the processed clearer type.

Quinoa: Quinoa provides all nine amino acids, making it a super-superfood, which will increase your protein intake and add fiber to your diet.

Oats, buckwheat, brown rice, and wild rice: These common whole grains are packed with antioxidants and vitamins and are a good source of soluble fiber, which can lower cholesterol levels and improve heart health. They also provide sustained energy. Be sure to choose whole grains over refined grains.

Nuts and seeds: Nuts and seeds are rich in fiber, protein, and heart-healthy fats. They also have anti-inflammatory and antioxidant properties, which can protect against oxidative stress and disease.

- **Nuts:** Walnuts, pecans, almonds, pistachios, hazelnuts, cashews, macadamia nuts, Brazil nuts, and more are very nutritious.

- **Seeds:** Sunflower seeds, pumpkin seeds, chia seeds, flaxseeds, hemp seeds, and other seeds provide protein and essential omega-3 fatty acids.

- **Nut butters and seed butters** offer the same benefits as nuts and seeds in an easier-to-digest form.

Sweet potatoes: This highly nutritious root vegetable is loaded with many nutrients, including potassium, fiber, vitamins A and C, and carotenoids, which have strong antioxidant properties.

Broccoli: Broccoli, Brussels sprouts, bok choy, cauliflower, cabbage, and other cruciferous vegetables can help lower the risk of cancer and prevent heart attacks and stroke. They also help maintain the balance of healthy bacteria in your gut and could reduce or prevent digestive conditions.

Fruits: Fruits such as oranges, apples, mangoes, pears, cherries, peaches, pineapple, plums, grapefruit, watermelon, lemons, and limes provide vitamins, fiber, antioxidants, and water.

Garlic: People have used nutrient-rich garlic, with its antibacterial and antiviral properties, to prevent or fight illnesses and infections since ancient times.

Greek Yogurt: Greek yogurt is rich in protein, probiotics, and calcium. It supports digestive health and bone health.

Fermented foods: Sauerkraut, pickles, yogurt, kimchi, kefir, kombucha, and miso are immunity-enhancing and promote gut health.

Ginger: Ginger has long been known to help digestion and manage nausea. You'll find it in basically all herbal teas for aiding digestion. You can also buy chewable ginger tablets or candied ginger pieces to improve digestion.

Green tea: Green tea is antioxidant-rich, with immunity-boosting properties and many other health benefits.

Dark chocolate: The cacao in dark chocolate is full of antioxidants, which may play a role in cancer prevention, heart health, and weight loss. Other benefits include improving cognition, preventing memory loss, and boosting your mood.

Avocado: Avocado is rich in healthy monounsaturated fats, fiber, and potassium. It supports heart health, aids digestion, and provides skin-nourishing benefits.

Chia Seeds: Chia seeds are packed with omega-3 fatty acids, protein, fiber, and antioxidants. They can help regulate blood sugar, promote satiety, and support digestive health.

Turmeric: Turmeric contains curcumin, a powerful anti-inflammatory compound. It may help reduce the risk of chronic diseases and alleviate joint pain.

Raw, unpasteurized honey: This superfood is packed with antioxidants, which fight free radicals, reduce oxidative damage, and protect against cellular aging and premature cell death, inflammation, and DNA damage.

Raw honey can also: fight infection, boost the immune system, aid digestion, reduce blood pressure, soothe sore throats and coughs, and provide quick energy.

Food Allergies and Intolerances

What is the difference between a food allergy and a food intolerance or sensitivity?

Food allergies: People with a food allergy have an immune response to allergens in specific foods and can develop serious symptoms like trouble breathing, rashes, and even anaphylaxis.

Food intolerances and sensitivities can cause digestive symptoms like gastrointestinal discomfort, bloating, gas, and diarrhea. Food intolerances and sensitivities can be more difficult to identify but are rarely life-threatening.

Food Allergens

The "Big 8" most common food allergens are:

1. Cow's milk

2. Eggs

3. Peanuts

4. Tree nuts (almonds, walnuts, cashews, etc.)

5. Shellfish

6. Wheat

7. Soy

8. Fish

Other, less common, allergens include sesame seeds and mustard.

Food Intolerances

Some common food intolerances include:

- Dairy (cow's milk) products

- Gluten (grains such as wheat, barley, rye, and more)

- Eggs, especially egg whites

- Caffeine

- Soybeans and soy products (edamame, tofu, miso, etc.)

- Peanuts

- Corn

- Salicylates (found in aspirin, coffee, lentils, and more)

- Amines, such as histamine (found in cured meat, processed seafood and poultry, and more)

- High FODMAP foods

- Sulfites

- Fructose

- Aspartame, an artificial sweetener

- Monosodium glutamate, or MSG, used as a flavor-enhancing additive in foods.

- Food colorings like Red 40 and Yellow 5

- Yeast

- Sugar alcohols, used as zero calorie alternatives to sugar.

If you suspect you have any food-related issues, be sure to check food ingredient labels and consult a healthcare professional for an accurate diagnosis and guidance.

Sources:

Healthline: https://www.healthline.com/nutrition/common-food-allergies

VeryWellHealth: Food Intolerance: Symptoms, Common Foods , Vs. Food Allergies (verywellhealth.com)

Food Allergy Canada, health.clevelandclinic.org, nutritionhealthworks.com.

Specific Dietary Needs of People with ME/CFS

In addition to the above important guidelines, it's especially critical for people with energy-limiting chronic conditions to be mindful of what we eat, how much, and how often.

We have specific dietary needs, according to Dr. Sarah Myhill. Here's a summary of most of her "Rules of the Diet Game," in order of priority in her excellent book, *Diagnosis and Treatment of Chronic Fatigue Syndrome and Myalgic Encephalitis*:

- No alcohol: 90% of ME/CFS sufferers are alcohol intolerant.

- Increase intake of healthy fat and fiber and decrease intake of starch and sugar.

- No sugar, no fruit sugar, nothing ending in *-ose*.

- No artificial sweeteners (stevia and xylitol are fine to use in moderation).

- Low-starch diet. Starches to be eaten only once a day, in moderate amounts.

- Cut out all foods containing gluten, dairy, and yeast.

- No cow's milk proteins (whey and casein).

- No hydrogenated fats (trans fats), such as margarine.

- Avoid added chemicals.

- Use caffeine in moderation.

- Chocolate: avoid milk chocolates loaded with sugar. Go for 70% or more cacao.

- Avoid nicotine.

- Eat organic as much as possible.

Common Food Sensitivities for People with ME/CFS

People with ME and/or fibromyalgia typically have difficulties digesting certain foods, and the resulting symptoms can exacerbate their condition.

According to an article called "Nutrition and Chemical Sensitivity" by Bruce Campbell, published on the website ME/CFS & Fibromyalgia Self-Help,

"Most people with ME/CFS and FM experience an intolerance of alcohol, and many are sensitive to other substances, including: caffeine and other stimulants; sweeteners such as sugar, corn syrup, fructose, aspartame and saccharin; food additives such as MSG, preservatives, artificial colors and artificial flavors; and tobacco."

Campbell advises that cutting down or eliminating these substances may reduce symptoms and improve sleep.

He states,

"About one third of people with ME/CFS and fibromyalgia experience food sensitivities or food allergies or have difficulty absorbing nutrients."

Some common food allergies or sensitivities include:

- Dairy products
- Eggs
- Soy
- Wheat
- Corn

Supplements to Help Increase Mitochondrial Function

To date, there appears to be no single supplement—or even combination—that will have you kicking up your heels. But an encouraging number of people with ME/CFS, long COVID, and fibromyalgia have found reduced symptoms and improvement in energy from certain over-the-counter capsules and tablets.

Here are five lists of supplements that have been shown to be beneficial, from five respected sources.

1. From the American Myalgic Encephalomyelitis and Chronic Fatigue Syndrome Society (https://ammes.org/supplements/):

"Nutritional supplements are an essential component of any ME/CFS treatment protocol. Research has shown that people with ME/CFS are routinely deficient in several important nutrients."

And even if you aren't deficient in them, "the demands of a chronic illness make it necessary to provide additional nutritional support— especially in light of the numerous GI problems prevalent in the ME/CFS population, which may lead to malabsorption. Most ME/CFS doctors recommend nutritional supplements as part of their protocols."

Note: It's best to take supplements in very small doses initially, one at a time, allowing three or four days in between, to test each for possible negative reactions or sensitivities. Also, supplements and vitamins should be taken with food, unless instructed otherwise.

Supplements can be expensive, but cheaper brands can be of poor quality and less effective. It's safest to purchase from well-known, respected brands.

Purchasing online, rather than from retail outlets, can cut the cost of expensive supplements in half.

Five commonly recommended supplements for ME/CFS patients, according to ammes.org:

- **Acetyl-L-Carnitine:** Carnitine deficiency produces fatigue, muscle weakness, malaise, exercise intolerance, heartbeat abnormalities, and tissue acidosis.

- **Antioxidants:** Alpha Lipoic Acid, Vitamin E, Vitamin C, etc. Antioxidants are a group of vitamins, minerals, and enzymes that help protect cells from free radical damage.

- **CoQ10 / Ubiquinol:** Coenzyme Q10 (ubiquinone) helps produce adenosine triphosphate (ATP), the cellular source of energy. CoQ10 appears to reduce fatigue, alleviate muscle weakness and pain, and reduce cognitive dysfunction.

- **Essential Fatty Acids:** Omega-3, Omega-6, EPA, DHA, Fish Oil, Flaxseed Oil, Evening Primrose Oil, Borage Seed Oil. Studies have found that ME/CFS patients benefit from supplementation with EFAs.

- **Vitamin B12:** Dr. Charles Lapp and Dr. Paul Cheney observed that B12 injections have been beneficial to their ME/CFS patients, even in the absence of vitamin B12 deficiency or any sign of anemia.

2. Dr. Lapp's Recommendations on Supplements

Dr. Charles Lapp, founder and medical director of the Hunter-Hopkins Center in Charlotte, North Carolina, which specializes in ME/CFS and FM, stresses that:

There is no cure so far for either ME/CFS or FM, but certain supplements may be used to optimize health and may produce modest improvement in some symptoms.

161

Dr. Lapp advises that people try only one new supplement at a time, keeping it if it works and dropping it if it is ineffective. Supplements usually take at least three weeks to produce maximum effect.

Here's a summarized list of Dr. Lapp's top eight recommended supplements:

A high-quality **multi-vitamin** that includes B complex, folate, vitamin D, calcium, and magnesium; **B12** (preferably the injectable form or sublingual); as well as **vitamin D3, D-Ribose, calcium, and magnesium.**

And for those struggling at a lower level, with less energy and more brain fog, Dr. Lapp recommends the addition of:

NADH "helps increase ATP in mitochondria"; and **Acetyl-carnitine** "often used with NADH to increase energy production" and "may improve cognition."

Similar Recommendations from Other Respected Sources:

3. Evan H. Hirsch, MD, ABOIM, in his book *Fix Your Fatigue*, recommends these "mitochondrial energy optimizers":

D-Ribose, acetyl-L-Carnitine, L-carnitine, NADH, alpha lipoic acid, glutathione, B vitamins, and CoQ10

4. Dr. Myhill's "mitochondrial package of supplements," from her book, *Diagnosis and Treatment of Chronic Fatigue Syndrome and Myalgic Encephalitis*, includes:

Co-Q10, niacinamide, acetyl L-carnitine, D-ribose, magnesium, glutathione, and vitamin B12

5. PainScale.com: "Supplement Options for Myalgic Encephalomyelitis/Chronic Fatigue Syndrome (ME/CFS)"

Supplements that may be beneficial to alleviate symptoms of ME/CFS include:

Coenzyme Q10, nicotinamide adenine dinucleotide (NAD), ribose / D-ribose, magnesium, B vitamins, and vitamin D

> **The six most recommended supplements** from the above lists by five reputable sources:
>
> **Co-Q10, D-Ribose, Vitamin B12, Magnesium, Acetyl-L-carnitine, and Vitamin D**

Important note: Of course, before you start taking a supplement, **be sure to check with your doctor or respected healthcare provider**, who can take into account your individual situation.

Digestion and Your Gut Microbiome

The term "gut health" refers to the health of the hundreds of different species of microorganisms that live in the large intestine and make up the gut microbiome.

According to Heather Jones, in her article, "Best and Worst Foods for Gut Health,"

- The gut microbiome bacteria help break down food for the body to use efficiently.

- Gut health is also linked to overall health.

- Approximately 70% of the body's immune system is in the gut.

- Gut health has also been associated with autoimmune diseases, gastrointestinal disorders, mental health, cardiovascular disease, and more.

The foods we eat affect our microbiome and in turn our gut health.

Depending on which foods we choose, they can either help promote a healthy gut microbiome or, conversely, deplete the helpful bacteria and increase the harmful bacteria. We need a rich, diverse microbiota to withstand external threats.

Best and Worst Foods for Digestion and Gut Health

Best Foods for a Healthy Gut

Some foods that are good for our gastrointestinal health:

Foods high in fiber

A high-fiber diet helps our digestion and absorption of nutrients, and also helps prevent constipation.

According to Jones, "It [fiber] has also been linked with a reduced risk of health conditions such as heart disease, type 2 diabetes, and colon cancer."

Foods that are high in fiber include:

Whole grains, vegetables, fruits, nuts, seeds, beans, peas, and lentils.

Some easy, high-fiber snacks:

- Granola, muesli, or other high-fiber cereal
- An apple
- Raw celery
- A handful of roasted nuts
- A handful of roasted sunflower or pumpkin seeds

Fermented Foods

"A diet rich in fermented foods has been associated with increased microbial diversity and may decrease some markers of inflammation."

Caution: High heat can kill the beneficial probiotics (live helpful microorganisms) in fermented foods, so be sure not to cook them on high heat.

Beneficial fermented foods include:

Yogurt, sauerkraut (choose refrigerated), kombucha, kimchi, tempeh, kefir, sourdough, miso, fermented vegetables, pickles (in salt, not vinegar), probiotic drinks, and certain aged cheeses (check the label).

Polyphenols

"Polyphenols are compounds found in plants that are not easily digested in the stomach. Microorganisms in the colon metabolize them. … polyphenols may promote helpful gut bacteria and inhibit invasive species." (H. Jones)

Sources of polyphenols include:

Fruits, vegetables, nuts, peanuts, and seeds, ginger, turmeric, red pepper flakes, soy products, coffee, green tea, black tea, dark chocolate, and cocoa.

Omega-3 Fatty Acids

"Omega-3 fatty acids may help restore balanced healthy microbiota, strengthen the gut wall, and decrease inflammatory microorganisms." (H. Jones)

Sources of omega-3 fatty acids (healthy fats) include:

Sardines, salmon, tuna, mackerel, and herring; nuts and seeds; olive oil, olives, avocados

Water

Getting enough liquids, especially water, is essential for gut health. Water helps gut health by assisting with the breakdown of food, softening stools, preventing constipation, and helping fiber do its job.

Foods to Limit or Avoid for a Healthy Gut

Ultra-Processed Foods

Try to eat foods that are as close to their natural state as possible.

Highly processed foods may contain added sugar, salt, and saturated or trans fats, as well as chemical additives, all of which can increase inflammation and negatively influence gut health.

Ultra-processed foods include:

Deli meats, many packaged snacks, many breakfast cereals, sweet desserts, and some ready-made meals.

Greasy Fried Foods

Fried foods, burgers, fries/chips, and other foods high in saturated fats can be difficult to digest and can lead to stomach upset such as heartburn.

Artificial Sweeteners

"Though more research is necessary, some evidence suggests that certain artificial sweeteners, including aspartame, sucralose, and saccharin, may negatively impact the balance and diversity of the gut microbiota." (H. Jones)

Caffeine and Alcohol

"These may increase inflammation, but they're also known to increase cortisol—a stress hormone that might overload your already exhausted body. [...] use them in moderation and be aware that they may trigger symptoms." (Adrienne Dellwo)

In summary, our choice of foods definitely impacts our gut health.

"Eating a diet that includes a wide variety of foods high in fiber, probiotics (such as fermented foods), polyphenols, and omega-3 fatty acids can help support gut health. Getting enough fluids, particularly water, is essential to keep the gut healthy." (H. Jones)

Eat these instead:

A quick recap of the best foods to eat for optimal gut health and digestion:

- **Fruits,** especially berries, cherries, and apples, for their polyphenols., as well as, for their digestive enzymes:

  Papaya contains a digestive enzyme called papain, commonly used as the main enzyme in digestive supplements.

  Pineapple is the only known food source of bromelain, which **digests protein**.

  I keep frozen pineapple chunks in my freezer and thaw some in the microwave to eat after a heavy meal. Note that heat and cooking destroy bromelain, so to aid digestion, just defrost the pineapple rather than heating it up.

- **Vegetables,** especially dark leafy greens, for their antioxidants.

- **Fish and Seafood,** especially salmon, mackerel, and sardines, for their omega-3 fats, which can reduce inflammation.

- **Nuts and Seeds,** especially walnuts, flax seeds (best as ground flax), and chia seeds, which, besides providing protein, are all great sources of omega-3 fats.

- **Fermented Foods** such as kefir, Greek yogurt, sauerkraut, kombucha, kimchi, tempeh, kefir, sourdough, miso, fermented vegetables, and pickles provide both beneficial bacteria and helpful probiotics.

- **Olive oil, olives, and avocados** also provide healthy fats.

- **Dark Chocolate** is a good source of polyphenols.

Resources for this chapter:

"Best and Worst Foods for Gut Health" by Heather Jones, VeryWellHealth, June 28, 2023.

"What to Eat When You Have Chronic Fatigue Syndrome" by Adrienne Dellwo, in CFS & Fibromyalgia – Living With.

Digestive Aids, Enzymes, Probiotics

Some Natural Digestive Aids

If you have indigestion or gas, you could try one of these home digestive aids:

- Ginger tea or any herbal tea that has ginger in it

- Crystallized or candied ginger

- Make your own ginger water. Boil one or two pieces of ginger root in 4 cups of water. Add flavor with lemon or honey before drinking. (Recipe from Healthline.)

- Peppermint tea

- Chamomile tea

- Apple cider vinegar. Never drink full strength! 1 to 2 teaspoons per cup of water is a good ratio. I add honey.

- Baking soda—¼ to ½ tsp dissolved in warm water

- Fennel seeds, fennel in tea

- Licorice root in tea

- Lemon water

- Pineapple

- Mango

Supplements to help digestion:

- Digestive enzymes

- Probiotics

- Ginger pills

170

Probiotics vs Digestive Enzymes

Should I take probiotics or digestive enzymes to help with indigestion?

According to an article called "Probiotics vs Digestive Enzymes – What's the Difference?" by Anna Gora in livescience.com, both supplements help improve gut health and aid digestion by efficiently breaking down food into nutrients.

"… digestive enzymes break down complex nutrients into smaller particles, while probiotics help to maintain a balance between the 'good' and the 'bad' gut bacteria. As such, they may treat or improve different digestive issues."

What are digestive enzymes?

Digestive enzymes are tiny protein molecules that your body makes to break down food into useable nutrients. These enzymes are produced in our salivary glands, stomach, small intestine, and pancreas.

Common types of digestive enzymes include amylase, lipase, protease, lactase, and sucrase, each of which breaks down different types of foods.

You can increase your body's production of digestive enzymes through supplements and by eating these foods: ginger, pineapples, papayas, mangoes, honey, bananas, kiwifruit, avocados; and fermented foods such as kefir, yogurt, sauerkraut, kimchi, and miso.

What are probiotics?

According to the article, "Probiotics are live bacteria and yeasts that can beneficially affect our health by improving the balance and function of gut bacteria." They are found naturally in the body, in probiotic foods like yogurt, kefir, miso soup, kimchi, sauerkraut and tempeh, and in probiotic supplements.

Probiotics vs Digestive Enzymes: Which Supplements Should You Take?

Both help with gas and bloating. In addition,

Digestive enzymes help with:

Indigestion, acid reflux, irregular bowel movements, nausea, frequent burping, feeling uncomfortably full after a meal, food sensitivities, and more.

Probiotics help with:

Irregular bowel movements, skin rashes, acne, eczema, anxiety, irritability, trouble concentrating, weak immune system, fatigue, aching joints, and more.

Can you take probiotics and digestive enzymes together?

According to Anna Gora, "The combination of digestive enzymes and probiotics is a safe approach to support healthy digestion. Although both enzymes and probiotics work in the gastrointestinal tract, they address different health issues and don't counteract each other."

Gora states that sometimes both enzymes and friendly bacteria are needed for optimal digestion and intestinal wellbeing.

However, it's always a good idea to consult your respected health provider before you start taking them.

You can usually manage minor, occasional indigestion problems with food choices and home remedies, including sauerkraut, pickles, pineapple, mangoes, ginger, and peppermint. But of course, indigestion that occurs more often or with other symptoms may need medical attention.

Note: This chapter is for informational purposes only and is not meant to offer medical advice.

Electrolytes

What are electrolytes?

Electrolytes are essential minerals that, when dissolved in water, create electrical charges that are vital to the body's functioning.

According to Healthline.com,

"Electrolytes are essential for keeping your nervous system and muscles functioning. They also ensure that your body's internal environment is optimal by keeping you hydrated and helping regulate your internal pH."

Everyone needs electrolytes to survive. Many automatic processes in the body rely on a small electric current to function, and electrolytes provide this charge.

Electrolytes interact with each other and the cells in the tissues, nerves, and muscles. A balance of different electrolytes is crucial for the body to function.

The most essential electrolytes include:

Calcium, chloride, magnesium, phosphate, potassium, sodium, and bicarbonate.

Why do we need electrolytes?

According to VeryWellHealth.com,

"Electrolytes are involved in practically everything your body does. They are present in blood plasma and inside cells, where they help to stabilize cell membranes.

"Electrolytes also maintain protein structure and fluid balance. Electrolytes play a role in chemical reactions in the body, and they help transport substances into and out of cells."

Getting the right balance of electrolytes is vital for human health.

What do electrolytes do?

According to MedicalNewsToday.com,

"Electrolytes play an essential role in many bodily functions and processes. They are important for:

- balancing blood pH and blood pressure
- ensuring adequate hydration
- facilitating the transfer of electrical impulses from the heart, muscle, and nerve cells to other cells
- helping fix tissue damage
- regulating nerve and muscle function, including muscle relaxation and contraction
- contributing to blood clotting"

Where do we find electrolytes?

Electrolytes in food

Many foods contain electrolytes, including:

Leafy green vegetables, other vegetables, fruits, dairy products, nuts, seeds, beans, lentils, table salt, salty foods, and some breakfast cereals.

Electrolytes in drinks

Some drinks are naturally rich in electrolytes, while others have undergone special formulation to provide electrolytes.

Some examples of electrolyte drinks:

- Coconut water (highest in a good variety of electrolytes and naturally low in sugar)

- Watermelon water and other fruit juices

- Cow's milk, soy milk

- Smoothies

- Electrolyte-infused waters

- Electrolyte tablets

- Electrolyte powder such as Liquid IV

- Sports drinks like Biosteel, Gatorade, Powerade

- Recovery drinks such as Pedialyte

Make your own electrolyte drink:

Mix together:

- 1 cup (8 ounces) herbal tea or hot water

- 1–2 tablespoons lemon juice

- Small pinch of salt

- 1 teaspoon honey (preferably raw, unpasteurized)

Note: Consuming the right number of electrolytes is vital for human health. Too few or too many electrolytes can contribute to an electrolyte imbalance.

It's best to speak to your doctor or pharmacist before taking electrolyte supplements.

Caution: Don't overdo the electrolytes.

A high intake of electrolytes can contribute to an electrolyte imbalance.

The symptoms of an electrolyte imbalance can include:

Twitching, weakness, nausea, vomiting, fatigue, confusion, fainting, and, if unchecked, seizures and heart rhythm disturbances.

If you experience these symptoms, seek medical help immediately.

Older adults are particularly at risk of an electrolyte imbalance.

Why Do People with ME/CFS Or Long Covid Especially Need Electrolytes?

People with Myalgic Encephalomyelitis/Chronic Fatigue Syndrome (ME/CFS), long COVID, or other fatigue conditions benefit from consuming electrolytes for several reasons:

Orthostatic Intolerance

Many people with ME/CFS experience orthostatic intolerance or POTS, which means their bodies have difficulty maintaining blood pressure and blood flow when they are in an upright position. Electrolytes, especially sodium and potassium, play a crucial role in regulating blood pressure and fluid balance, which can help alleviate symptoms of orthostatic intolerance such as dizziness, lightheadedness, and fatigue.

Dehydration

When we're fatigued, we may not have the energy to drink enough water and other fluids. Dehydration can worsen our fatigue, muscle pain, and cognitive problems. Electrolytes help the body retain water and maintain proper fluid balance, reducing the risk of dehydration.

Energy Production

Electrolytes are essential for various biological processes, including the production of cellular energy. People with ME/CFS usually experience reduced energy levels, so adequate electrolyte levels can help increase cellular energy production and overall well-being.

Muscle Function

Electrolytes, particularly calcium, sodium, and potassium, are vital for proper muscle function. People with ME/CFS may experience muscle weakness and pain, and maintaining proper electrolyte levels can help reduce muscle cramps and discomfort.

Gastrointestinal Symptoms

Some people with ME/CFS experience digestive problems that result in diarrhea and vomiting, causing a loss of bodily fluids and leading to electrolyte imbalances. Replenishing electrolytes can help reduce these symptoms and maintain electrolyte balance.

Bottom line: It's important for people with ME/CFS, long COVID, and other conditions characterized by low energy and muscle weakness to make sure you're getting enough electrolytes. But be cautious of not overdoing it.

Note: Be sure to consult with your healthcare provider before adding any supplements to your diet, including electrolytes. Your healthcare professional can provide guidance on the appropriate type and dosage of electrolyte supplements (as well as other supplements) based on your specific needs and health status.

Sources:

Healthline.com, MedicalNewsToday.com, VeryWellHealth.com

RECIPES

"It's not meal planning, you're life planning." – Nature's Fare Markets

In this chapter, you'll find a limited selection of recipes that are all easy to prepare for those low on energy. The focus here is on simple, nutritious, tasty dishes with ingredients we have on hand or are easy to find.

All of the recipes are low in sugar, unhealthy fats, and refined grains, and high in superfoods and other nutritious, energy-supplying ingredients.

Because many people with ME/CFS have food sensitivities and intolerances, many of the recipes are dairy-free and gluten-free.

(As an aside, I have food sensitivities to dairy and gluten, but can manage small amounts of both. In the case of dairy, cow's milk and soft cheese give me stomach discomfort, but I can easily digest yogurt and aged, hard cheese, probably because of the fermenting process they go through.)

Breakfast Ideas

Smoothie

Nutritious, delicious, and packed with protein. Also, easy to digest.

To a blender, add frozen mixed berries (or other fruit), banana, Greek yogurt, protein powder, spinach or kale, and water. Blend and enjoy.

Smoothie bowl

Make the above (or another) smoothie without the water (or just a little). Pour/spoon the thick mixture into a bowl and add granola or muesli. Can also add more berries or chopped fruit, shredded coconut, or toasted chopped nuts or seeds.

Quick & Easy Power Toast

Toast a slice or two of whole wheat, multigrain, sourdough, or gluten-free bread and spread with peanut butter or other nut butter. Top with sliced bananas or sprouts.

Eggs

Two eggs any style with 2 slices whole-grain toast will give you 20 g of protein. Add some sliced oranges or other fruit on the side. I find scrambled eggs to be the easiest. You can even scramble them in the microwave.

To make it gluten-free, choose gluten-free bread or rice crackers.

Optional: For more protein, you could add high-protein milk, cottage cheese (if you can tolerate it), nutritional yeast, or protein powder to the scrambled eggs.

Yogurt–Granola Parfait

Layer sugar-free plain or vanilla yogurt, blueberries, strawberries, or mixed berries (thawed if frozen) and granola or muesli in two or three layers. Enjoy!

Note: For added protein, use Greek yogurt. Three-quarters of a cup of 2% Greek yogurt with berries and 1/4 cup sliced almonds or 1/3 cup granola or muesli will give you 21 g of protein.

Overnight oats

I bought some glass jars with lids from the dollar store and make four or five jars of overnight oats at a time. They keep well for up to five days in the fridge. I vary them a bit at the time of making or before I eat them.

Here's the basic recipe I use. One half cup of oats makes a bit too much, but rather than using 1/3 cup oats, I prefer to make a little more to have some left over for a mid-morning snack.

Overnight Oats:

In each jar, add in this order:

- 1/2 cup large-flake (old-fashioned) rolled oats
- 1 Tbsp chia seeds
- 1–2 tsp protein powder (optional)
- 1–2 Tbsps chopped walnuts or sliced almonds
- 1/4 cup Greek yogurt
- 2 pinches (or shakes) of salt (to taste)
- 1 Tbsp maple syrup or honey (optional)Si
- 3/4 cup milk of choice (almond, rice, oat, cashew, coconut, etc.)

Stir well, cover, and let sit in fridge overnight.

Before eating, can add berries, fruit, chopped nuts, or granola on top.

Note: I have found that large-flake oats work best. Quick oats result in a mushy texture, and of course stone-cut oats won't work.

Big-Batch Hearty Oatmeal

Make a big pot of oatmeal and eat for 4-5 days.

Bring 4 cups of water to boil and add:

- 2 cups quick or large-flake oats
- ½–1 tsp salt
- ½ tsp vanilla extract
- 1/4 cup raisins or dried cranberries
- 1/3–1/2 cup chopped walnuts

- Handful of sunflower or pumpkin seeds (or both)

Optional: Add flax seeds or other nuts or seeds for extra protein

Variation: Chopped apple, chopped walnuts, and ½ tsp cinnamon

Mix well and stir regularly until cooked.

When serving, you can add maple syrup or brown sugar to taste and blueberries or other berries.

Apple-Walnut Slow-Cooker Oats

Ingredients:

- 4 cups water
- 2 cups large-flake oats (quick oats not recommended)
- 1 small apple, cored, quartered, and chopped into small pieces
- 1/3 cup walnuts, chopped
- ½ tsp salt
- ½ tsp vanilla
- ½ tsp cinnamon
- ¼ cup coconut sugar or brown sugar or maple syrup, optional

Instructions: Spray the inside of the cooker with a non-stick cooking spray or grease with butter. Better yet, line the slow cooker with parchment paper or a slow-cooker liner you can throw out after.

Add all ingredients to slow cooker, stir well, and cook on high for 1 ½ hours. I stir it a few times while it's cooking. Or can cook on low for longer.

Egg and Veggie Muffins

Whip up a batch of these, then eat a few with toast, rice crackers, or fruit. Refrigerate or freeze the rest, then take out, heat in microwave for 60 seconds, and enjoy.

This recipe is for 6 egg muffins, but it's easy to just double the recipe to make a dozen.

Ingredients:

- 6 large eggs
- 2 tbsp (1/8 cup) milk of your choice
- 1/2 cup chopped fresh spinach (or frozen)
- 1/3 cup quartered cherry tomatoes or chopped red pepper
- 1/4 cup diced onions (frozen is fine) or chopped green onions
- 1/3 cup chopped broccoli or zucchini
- Seasoning to taste
- Optional: top with grated cheese

Instructions:

1. Preheat the oven to 350°F. Grease a muffin tin with cooking spray.
2. In a large bowl, whisk together the eggs, milk, and seasonings of your choice (salt, pepper, etc.)
3. Stir in all the chopped vegetables.
4. Divide the mixture evenly between 6-8 muffin pan cups.
5. Bake for 20-25 minutes, or until the egg is fully cooked.
6. Remove from the oven. Add a sprinkle of grated cheese if desired, then let cool for 5 minutes in the pan.
7. Serve, refrigerate, or freeze.

Banana Protein Pancakes for One or Two (Gluten-free)

Ingredients

- 1 ripe banana, mashed
- 2 eggs

- 1/3 cup oats
- 1/2 tsp cinnamon
- Optional: 1 tsp to 1 tbsp protein powder

Directions

1. In bowl, beat eggs into the mashed banana.

2. Blend oats and cinnamon together until fine, then add to the bowl and stir well.

3. For each pancake, pour 1/4 cup of batter into skillet at medium heat and cook for about 60-90 seconds on each side until golden brown.

Serve with nut butter for added protein and healthy fat.

Baked Sweet Potato Topped with Greek Yogurt & Chopped Walnuts

A delicious breakfast or snack that provides 9 g of protein.

Ingredients:

- 1 sweet potato
- 1/4 cup plain Greek yogurt
- 1 tablespoon chopped walnuts or 1/4 cup granola

Pierce the sweet potato with a fork in several places.

Cook in microwave 3–7 min (until a fork goes all the way in).

Split open lengthwise and top the two halves with Greek yogurt and chopped walnuts or granola.

Lunch Ideas

Salads

Yummy Chicken Salad – Mix chopped or shredded chicken, grapes, chopped celery, frozen peas, and olive oil mayo or yogurt to taste.

Jodie's Jazzed-up Coleslaw

- 1 bag of coleslaw with grated carrots
- 1 chopped apple
- Diced pineapple, drained. Save juice.
- Chopped walnuts
- Cranberries or currants
- Coleslaw dressing or poppyseed dressing
- A bit of pineapple juice
- A bit of lemon juice

Mix all ingredients together and store in fridge.

Best to make it a day ahead or at least 3-4 hours before serving.

Much better the second day.

Soups

To increase the nutrition of canned or prepared soups:

- Cook frozen chopped mixed veggies in a little water. When cooked, add the soup and continue to heat.
- Stir in some spinach or kale (fresh or frozen)
- To add more protein:
    - Stir in a tablespoon of nutritional yeast.
    - Whisk in an egg.

- o Add chicken pieces.
- o Add chopped ham.

Jodie's Easy, Nutritious, Thick Soup – a meal in itself

Ingredients:

- 1 carton Ramen broth (sold near the chicken and vegetable broths)
- Chopped zucchini or broccoli (or other veggies of choice)
- Frozen peas
- Spinach or kale
- Ramen rice noodles
- 2 eggs
- Optional: 1 can creamed corn
- Shredded or chopped chicken

Instructions:

1. In medium pot, combine ramen broth & zucchini or broccoli.
2. Cook for a while.
3. Add frozen peas, spinach or kale, and ramen rice noodles.
4. Cook for a while.
5. Whisk 2 eggs and whisk into broth.
6. Optional: Add 1 can creamed corn.
7. Add cooked shredded or chopped chicken. Stir and serve.

Quick individual "pizza"

Spread a pita round with tomato sauce, pizza sauce, or salsa. Sprinkle on some chopped broccoli or zucchini, diced onions, chopped red pepper, and diced ham, chicken, or tuna. Top with grated cheese. Heat in toaster oven or air fryer, or in oven under broiler.

Veggie and Hummus Pita or Wrap

Ingredients

- Pocket pita or soft tortilla
- 3 tablespoons hummus, and/or
- 1/4 avocado, mashed
- 1/2 cup mixed salad greens
- 1/4 red bell pepper, sliced, or sliced tomato
- 1/4 cup sliced cucumber or celery
- Alfalfa sprouts or other sprouts (optional)

Directions

Cut the pita in half and open the pocket of one side. Spread the inside of the pita with hummus (and avocado if you have it on hand). Add the vegetables and enjoy!

Alternatively, spread the hummus on a soft tortilla, add the veggies, and roll up.

Feel free to mix it up with different flavors of hummus and different types of vegetables, depending on your mood. Also, for additional protein, you could opt to add cheese, chickpeas, or any meat or canned fish you have around.

For two people, double this recipe.

Quinoa Veggie Nut Salad

First, buy a bag of cooked quinoa and some frozen chopped stir-fry vegetables such as onion, red pepper, and mushrooms. (Or, if you have the energy, prepare your own fresh vegetables.)

1. Steam or sauté the vegetables in olive oil.

2. Combine with cooked quinoa and one or two of these, toasted: walnuts, almonds, pine nuts, pecans, sunflower seeds, pumpkin seeds.

3. Toss with Italian salad dressing.

4. Eat fresh, warm or cold. Keeps well refrigerated.

Salmon Wrap

Place canned Alaskan boneless skinless salmon on a whole grain wrap. Add chopped avocado, tomatoes, greens, and plain yogurt. Wrap tightly, cut in half, and serve.

Dinner/Supper

If you have a slow cooker, instant cooker, or air fryer, they should have come with lots of good recipes that you can adapt to make them easier and/or healthier. Or you can google recipes for your small, energy-saving appliances. A rice cooker is also a great energy and time saver.

Quick Home-Cooked Microwave Meals

Loaded Sweet Potato

Ingredients:

- 1 medium or large sweet potato
- Can of chili

  Optional:
- Sour cream or shredded cheese
- Sliced green onion
- Sliced avocado

Instructions:

1. Scrub the sweet potato and poke several times with a fork.

2. Cook on a plate in the microwave oven until fork pierces to middle.

3. Remove and split in half. Cut down the middle of each half. Or score and mash the cooked sweet potato, leaving shell intact.

4. Load with chili or topping of choice.

5. Optional: Add sour cream, sliced green onion, chopped avocado, grated cheese.

Loaded Baked Potato

Scrub medium or large potato and poke several times with a fork.

Bake on a plate in microwave oven until soft.

Slice vertically down the middle, almost to the bottom. Or if large, split in half to make two.

Add cottage cheese or Greek yogurt or sour cream and sliced green onions or chopped cooked broccoli or thawed green peas.

Baking, Desserts, and Treats

In order to feel better and have more energy, we people with energy-limiting conditions need to cut way back on our sugar consumption. Most of us also need to reduce carbs and gluten.

Quick and Easy Healthy Desserts

- Thaw some frozen mango chunks, pineapple, or cherries in a dessert dish in the microwave oven.

- Have a snack cup of mandarin oranges or fruit cocktail.

- Or try pears, peaches, or fruit cocktail canned in water or juice. Avoid fruit canned in heavy syrup.

- Start with a jar of unsweetened applesauce or buy in the individual cups.
  - Spoon one cup into a dessert dish and add a teaspoon of chia seeds. Let sit for 10-15 minutes to thicken into a pudding.
  - Or mix the unsweetened applesauce with plain yogurt.
  - All three mixed together are delicious too.

Tips for enjoying special treats:

- Enjoy an occasional piece of cake (almost) guilt-free. Just scrape all or most of the icing off. Or maybe just leave a very thin layer on for taste.
- When you have a slice of pie, remove and set aside the edge crust at the top.
- Top a piece of cake or pie with plain yogurt instead of ice cream.

Every little bit helps to gradually reduce your sugar intake and feel better.

Yummy Chia Seed Pudding

Makes 3–4 servings.

Ingredients:

- 1 cup of chopped mangos, pears, or peaches (fresh, frozen, or canned) or snack cup of chopped fruit or fruit cocktail
- 3/4 cup almond milk or coconut milk
- 1/4 cup plain yogurt*
- 1/4 tsp cinnamon
- 1 Tbsp maple syrup

- 1/4 cup chia seeds

Directions

1. Combine all ingredients together in a blender and blend until smooth.

2. Partition into 3 or 4 small bowls or mini mason jars. Cover with wrap or seal with jar lids.

3. Allow mixture to soak overnight to thicken into a pudding consistency (minimum 2 hours if you want to eat them the same day).

Optional: When serving, can top with toasted sliced almonds, shredded coconut, berries, or extra cut-up fruit. Don't add the optional toppings until just prior to eating; otherwise, they will go soggy.

*If you don't eat or have yogurt, increase the milk to 1 cup.

Guilt-Free Chocolate-Nut Pick-Me-Up

- Large bar of dark chocolate (70-85% cocoa)

- Chopped nuts of choice

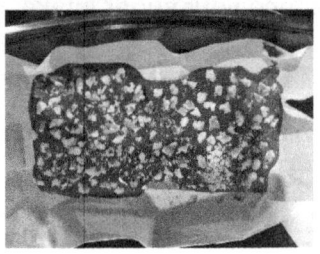 

1. Find a microwave-safe container about the same shape and size of the chocolate bar (like the ones individual microwave meals come in). Line it with parchment paper, extending up the sides.

2. Place the chocolate bar on the parchment paper and heat just until soft – not melted! – (use 20–30-second increments) in the microwave oven.

3. Sprinkle chopped nuts of your choice all over the top of the soft chocolate bar. Press the nuts down to embed them in the chocolate.

4. Heat a bit longer in the microwave.

5. Remove and store in refrigerator until firm.

6. Break up and store in a closed container in the fridge.

7. Remove just enough at a time from the fridge to eat right away, as the chocolate will soften too much at room temperature.

Easy Banana Ice Cream

Slice two (or more) ripe but still firm bananas and layer on cookie sheet to freeze. Remove from freezer and blend in food processor until creamy.

Could also add any frozen berries you have on hand.

Easy Keto Chocolate Dessert

Two-minute, no-flour, microwave recipe.

Serves 1–2 people.

Ingredients:

- 1 egg
- 2 tbsp almond milk (or any other milk)
- 2 tsp peanut butter, softened in microwave (optional)
- 2 tbsp cocoa powder
- 1 tbsp maple syrup, honey, or sweetener of your choice
- 1 tsp baking powder
- 1/2 tsp vanilla extract

Instructions:

1. Whisk all ingredients together.

191

2. Pour the mixture into a greased microwave-safe mug, ramekin, or small bowl.

3. Heat in microwave at maximum power for about 2 minutes.

Easy Yummy Rice Pudding

Delicious, gluten-free, and dairy-free

Uses pouches of cooked rice from store

In a crockpot or medium saucepan, add:

- 2 coconut-flavored jasmine rice pouches, well squeezed/kneaded to break up the rice

- I carton almond or coconut milk (or milk of choice)

- 1/2 medium apple, chopped small

- Dried cranberries or raisins or currants to taste

- 1/2 tsp cinnamon

- 1 tsp vanilla

- Pinch of salt

- Maple syrup to taste

- Optional, for added protein: finely chopped or ground almonds or other nuts (I use my coffee grinder to ground them.)

In pot, stir together until thickened.

In slow cooker, cook on high for 2 hours, stirring occasionally.

Tip for Easier Cookies

To make any cookie recipe quicker and easier, line a cake pan with parchment paper, hanging over the edges. Instead of making individual cookies, spread the mixture in the pan and bake for 30-40 minutes. Let cool on rack for 5 minutes, then slice into squares. I use a pizza slicer. Then lift the parchment paper and continue cooling out of the pan on a rack. Remove squares from parchment paper with lifter and store in fridge or freezer.

Using silicone baking pans also saves work.

GF, DF Oat, Banana, Applesauce Cookies

Gluten-Free, Dairy-Free, Healthy Cookies – No Sugar or Flour

Ingredients:

- 3 mashed ripe bananas
- 1/3 cup applesauce (preferably unsweetened)
- 2 cups quick oats
- 1/4 cup almond milk (or oat or cashew or milk of your choice)
- 1/4 –1/2 cup walnuts
- 1/2 cup raisins, dried cranberries, or dark chocolate chunks or chips
- 1 tsp vanilla
- 1 tsp cinnamon

Directions:

- Preheat oven to 350 degrees.
- Mix all ingredients together.
- Drop by spoonsful onto baking sheet.
- Bake for 15-20 minutes.

No-Bake Energy Bites

Ingredients:

- 1 cup quick oats
- 1/2 cup shredded coconut
- 1/2 cup ground nuts or ground flaxseeds

- 1/2 cup mini chocolate chips or sunflower seeds

- 1/2 cup nut butter, warmed to soften

- 1/3 cup honey

- 1 tsp vanilla extract

Directions:

1. Mix dry ingredients.

2. Add wet ingredients and mix well with a stand mixer or by hand.

3. Refrigerate for 30 minutes.

4. Use a cookie or ice cream scoop to scoop into balls, then roll a bit tighter.

5. Store in fridge in airtight container for 1-2 weeks or freeze for up to 3 months.

SUPPORT & RELATIONSHIPS

Helping Others Understand Your Condition

If you have ME/CFS (chronic fatigue syndrome), long covid, or any other energy-limiting condition, ask those close to you to read this book, especially the chapter for family and friends. Or search the condition online.

Easy Analogies

Not only do we have less physical and cognitive energy than our healthy friends and family members, but a healthy person will usually feel refreshed after a good night's sleep, whereas people with ME/CFS typically have non-refreshing sleep. So we may wake up as tired as or more fatigued than when we went to bed.

How can you easily describe to your family, friends, and others the limitations of your daily and weekly energy so they don't expect you to keep up with them or function like you did before?

Instead of saying, "I'm tired," or "I don't think I'll have the energy to do that," you can choose one of these analogies to help people understand your present energy level:

- **"My body battery is low."** Talk about their phone battery and say your body battery only charges to 10, 20, 30, or 40%, depending on your condition. And it drains much faster than their phone battery.

- **"I'm about to exceed my energy envelope for today."** You could put some coins in an envelope and take out coins until there are only one or two left.

- **"My body car is almost out of gas."** A healthy person will wake up with their body car full of gas, but your gas tank never fills up all the way, and it drains much faster than theirs.

- **"I only have two spoons left today."** (See the next page for an explanation of the spoon theory.)

- **"My energy bank account is almost overdrawn."** Tell them your body bank account has a limited amount of money in it for the day or week, and everyday activities can use up that money very quickly.

Balance energy withdrawals with energy deposits.

Energy deposits into your body bank/battery/car are:

- frequent rests
- hydration
- nutritious foods
- calming techniques
- positive thoughts

Energy withdrawals are:

- work
- stress/anxiety
- overexertion

We need to continually be mindful of increasing our deposits and reducing our withdrawals.

Another popular way to represent energy limitations is the number of spoonsful of energy we have for each day and how quickly they get used up.

Spoon Theory

In this analogy, your total energy for the day (which varies from person to person and day to day) can be indicated by a number of spoons, with each spoon representing a unit of energy.

Healthy people have significantly more "spoons" (energy) than those with a chronic fatigue condition. A healthy person could have, say, 20 to 30 spoons, whereas someone with chronic fatigue may have 6 to 12.

Some activities cost more spoons than others. For example, for someone with ME/CFS, brushing their teeth might take 1 spoon, and emptying the dishwasher or doing laundry could take 3 or 4 spoons. For some people, just taking a shower could take 4 or 5 or more of a daily allotment of 12 spoons.

So you need to make decisions about how to spend your limited number of spoons and reduce the number of spoons each chore takes. This book has plenty of tips for easier ways to accomplish everyday tasks, so you have more spoons left for activities we enjoy.

Of course, the number of spoons required to carry out any activity varies from person to person and day to day.

Personally, I find using the spoon analogy a bit too complicated and cumbersome, so I prefer to just think about my body battery draining, which my Garmin watch tracks and illustrates for me on the app. I find that visual reminder so much easier.

On the other hand, others with energy impairment find the phrase "I don't have the spoons for that" a quick and easy way to express how they're feeling.

How to Keep Your Support System

You need your friends and allies.

Life can be lonely if you're housebound or bedbound. And calling up an old friend to chat can seem like a mammoth undertaking, considering your limited energy and the other things you need to get done on any given day. Even detailed emailing or texting can be tiring.

Also, you're likely no longer able to attend events you used to love participating in, where you also had an opportunity to socialize. As a result, your former social networks and large circle of acquaintances may have dwindled down to just a few close friends and family members.

Be careful not to alienate your friends.

We all need our support systems, so whether you're talking to close friends or casual acquaintances, it's important not to alienate them by too much negativity or complaining. Let's face it, most human beings are basically selfish. We're wired that way for survival.

Remember that people around you have their own problems and needs.

It's easy to think everyone else's life is perfect compared to yours, but everyone has problems they're dealing with. And they're busy with their own lives. They don't necessarily have the time, maturity, or empathy to fully understand your conditions and limitations.

But do educate your close friends and family members about your condition.

Close friends and family need to know your current state and limitations, so they don't place too many unreasonable demands on you. The stress and/or exertion from dealing with unfair demands could easily exacerbate your condition.

199

So tell them how you're feeling in a matter-of-fact way, and explain that you can't actually manage what they're asking or suggesting. Then change the subject.

How to deal with acquaintances and casual friends.

Try to stay as positive as possible in interactions with casual or former friends. Approach it as providing information on your condition rather than complaining about it.

If you're chatting with a friend you only see occasionally, and they ask how you're doing, tell them your limitations and current reality in a kind of abbreviated way, then ask about their life and family or mutual friends. You'll find they have problems too. That approach will keep the lines of communication open between you and ensure that they look forward to chatting with you again.

Keep it brief and matter of fact.

If they're casual friends, don't go into a lot of detail, but let them know matter-of-factly that you can no longer play sports, go on long walks or hikes with them, attend parties, or whatever.

It can be hard to know to what extent discussion about a problem is okay or not okay with someone. Some people feel uncomfortable hearing about someone's problems because they don't know what to say or don't want their own mood to deteriorate.

Let them know your limitations so they don't continue to make unreasonable demands on you.

If people know about your condition, it helps them understand what you're going through, which can be beneficial. They're likely to stop expecting you to do things you're no longer able to manage, which will let off pressure on you.

It's best to be honest about your condition but focus on information and solutions rather than complaints.

If people actually want to know how you feel on your worst days, you could say something like this:

"Imagine you've got the worst hangover you've ever had, combined with the flu, and it goes on for weeks."

Offer a compromise, if you're able.

If you're invited to a wedding, for example, but you know the ceremony, dinner, and dance would be too much, you could say something like, "I'm happy for you and want to celebrate your wedding. If I'm feeling well, I plan to come for the [ceremony/dinner/whatever]."

That way, you're being honest and informative but offering a positive solution. That's better than saying, "I'm just too sick to come," which might make them think it's just an excuse or feel badly about inviting you. They may even stop inviting you to events or even calling you. So offer an alternative or decline in a way that's most likely to preserve your relationship.

Tips for handling the naysayers and disbelievers:

When dealing with doubting or even critical family or friends who might say, "Everyone gets tired," or "Just get out and get some exercise," it's best to stay calm. Try to keep your frustration and anger in check. Stress will only worsen your condition. Be armed with the facts from respected websites and this book.

Socializing, Visitors, and Guests

Phone Conversations

When you're really tired or in a crash, even talking to a family member or close friend can be exhausting. Here are some suggestions:

- Tell people in advance that you find talking on the phone too tiring.
- Give them specific times when chatting on the phone works best for you.
- As soon as you answer, say something like, "Hi. Good to hear from you. Unfortunately, today I can only talk for 15 (5/10/20) minutes."

Socializing in Public

If you have to go to a social gathering (and you actually have the energy to go), plan ways to minimize the stress and exhaustion.

Before accepting, find out about the venue. If it's going to be too loud and have too much stimulation, politely decline.

If you accept, plan ahead. Plan an exit strategy for leaving early or as soon as you start to feel overwhelmed.

When there, focus on the people closest to you—the people you know the best—and tune out the rest.

Take breaks. Take washroom breaks or slip outside for a while to decompress.

Entertaining at Home

Having a Friend or Relative over for Coffee, Lunch, or Dinner

If you're thinking of inviting someone over, it's best to start with one person only—someone you know well—and make it coffee, tea, or lunch, not dinner.

Keep it simple, with minimum fuss to conserve your energy.

If you're starting with a coffee or tea visit, buy some cookies or other light snack and tell them in advance that unfortunately you'll only be good for about an hour (or 2 hours or 45 minutes or whatever). If they have a busy life, that will work for them too.

If it's lunch, plan something simple and tell them it will be basic.

If they offer to bring something, do accept.

Be sure to pace yourself.

Don't leave everything until the last minute, or you'll be too tired to enjoy your company or even so exhausted that you have to cancel. And that's disappointing to everyone. (Speaking from personal experience here.)

Do your tidying, cleaning, and shopping several days before, and plan to rest most of the day before.

Don't rush around getting everything ready just before they arrive. They can watch or help you set the table, get things out of the fridge, etc.

Conversation and Interaction

Carrying on a conversation is often exhausting.

Talking with someone, while it can be interesting and rewarding, is draining to most of us, as we try to focus on what's being said, process it, then come up with an appropriate response.

Prepare them in advance.

It might be best to gently inform your visitor(s) before or when they arrive that you can't focus as well as you used to, so following a conversation can sometimes/often be challenging for you.

What to talk about?

If your guests are family or close friends, conversation will usually come naturally. If it's someone you don't see as often, you might wonder what you'll talk about. Maybe you're afraid you'll bore them, and they won't want to come back or invite you to their place. Or perhaps you feel you don't have anything exciting to say because you no longer go out much.

- Ask them about their lives and try to be a good listener.

- If you follow the news, watch interesting shows on TV, or enjoy interesting books, you could chat about that.

- And of course, you can talk about people you know in common.

- Or show them a hobby you've been doing when you have the energy.

- Another option is to meet in a nearby park so you can chat about what's around you.

- Try to avoid complaining about your life, as your friends may make excuses to themselves (even subconsciously) to not spend time with you in the future.

Out-of-Town Overnight Guests

Clarify expectations to avoid disappointment and misunderstandings.

If you're expecting a guest to come and stay with you for several days, let them know in advance that you won't be able to go for long walks, sightsee all day, go to noisy restaurants, or entertain them as in past visits. Make sure they know that you'll need to rest a lot. Tell them to bring a book, an e-reader, or their tablet to amuse themselves when you're resting. Or they can go for walks or drives or watch TV quietly. Tell them about anything interesting in walking distance from your home, such as a pleasant park or some enjoyable sights or shops.

Also, let them know they're in charge of getting their own breakfast (in case you need to sleep in) and making and unmaking their bed. Leave them some clean bed linens on the bed.

Make it clear you won't be able to participate in everything.

If they want to be on the go all the time, give them your blessing to go without you. You could lend guests your car if you're too tired to drive them or even too tired to be a passenger. They need to know all of this in advance, so they come prepared to accommodate your energy levels and amuse themselves if necessary. This way, their expectations will be more realistic, and they won't be disappointed.

Chatting and catching up.

While they're visiting with you at your home, tell them that you'll be good for only about 15 to 20 minutes of conversation before needing a rest of 15 to 30 minutes (or whatever your limits are).

You can always watch a feel-good movie together. Avoid one with lots of loud noise and violence or a convoluted mystery that's too hard to follow. Or just watch one or two episodes of a series you both like. Buy a few snacks in advance for movie time.

Can't handle overnight guests?

If you're just too exhausted to have guests stay overnight at your home but still want to see them, your could suggest a nearby motel or airbnb. If you know you'll need lots of rest time, you could suggest a lodging close to a nice park or interesting galleries or shops so they can amuse themselves while you nap.

Or just say no.

Having overnight guests can be stressful and exhausting. There's no shame in saying you are not able to entertain house guests. It's best to just be honest and upfront when a potential guest first asks.

Remind yourself that **it's okay to say no**. Pleasing others isn't self-care, and you need to be all about self-care in order to survive and improve.

VENTURING OUT AND TRAVEL

Essentials for Leaving the House

Take What You Need When Going Out

Some suggestions:

- Your phone, keys, and wallet or purse
- Earplugs (in case you find yourself in a noisy place)
- Sunglasses, hat
- Water bottle
- Protein snack
- Card with a list of emergency contacts, meds, doctor
- Cane (walking stick) or a collapsible one for your purse or car
- If you need it, a rollator (four-wheel) walker with a basket or carry bag

Keep these in your vehicle:

- Sunglasses
- Hat with a visor
- Water bottle
- Healthy snacks
- Pen and paper
- Cleansing wipes
- Cane or collapsible cane
- Change of clothes and underwear
- Towel

- Small blanket

- Urine container (if it's a long drive and you think you might need it)

- Extra sweater or jacket

- Comfortable shoes or sandals

Also, if you have trouble standing for more than a few minutes, keep a lightweight, retractable, height-adjustable, portable stool for when you need to sit and no sitting options are available. It's especially useful for standing in lineups.

Out for dinner at a restaurant

- Choose a relatively quiet restaurant or at least a quiet section.

- Choose a booth if possible, so you can lean against the wall if needed and put your legs on the padded bench.

- If you have a portable chair back, consider taking that for added support and comfort at a table. If it's high, you can lean your head against it.

Going to a movie

- Try to choose a movie theater that has recliner seats so you can lean back a little, with your feet raised. Ahhh…game changer!

- Take earplugs for the loud previews! That's a must for me.

- Take water or a sports drink and a snack.

Going on a Trip

Don't forget these essentials when going away:

- Eye mask

- Earplugs

- Meds, vitamins, supplements

- Baby wipes or no-rinse body wipes

- Your favorite snacks and tea bags

- Warm socks

- Neck pillow

- Throw or cardigan

- Small flashlight

- Nightlight

- Clothes peg for keeping hotel room curtains closed

- Phone and charger

- Tablet and charger (if you use one often)

- Smartwatch and charger

- Maybe extra eyeglasses

- Small personal first-aid kit

- Cane or whatever mobility aid you might need

Air Travel

Here are some tips for making a long trip by airplane as stress-free as possible:

Booking your flight

Book the highest class you can afford, or at least a window seat so you can lean on the window to rest or sleep. Some people recommend the exit row for more leg room, but then what will you prop your feet on? They won't allow you to leave luggage in that space – it needs to be under your seat.

Arrange in advance for a wheelchair in the airport.

You can usually book that online when booking your flight. If you need it, request special assistance, which will take you through security and right to the plane in a wheelchair.

Consider booking access to an **airport lounge** to relax before the flight.

Packing

Get all your packing done and ready to go at least two days before you leave. If you need a cane at times, pack a fold-up one in your suitcase or carry-on case.

Set out what you'll wear on the plane.

Wear comfortable loose or stretchy clothes and comfy shoes, and layer, so you can take off a jacket or cardigan if you get too hot, or vice versa. Take socks and even slippers, if you like. Be sure to wear compression stockings if it's a long flight.

Avoid last-minute rushing around.

Plan everything in advance, so you can spend the day (or two) before you leave resting up for the trip.

Include these in your carry-on bag:
211

Your meds, a neck pillow (travel pillow), an eye mask, earplugs or noise-canceling headphones, a face mask (to avoid picking up a virus), an empty plastic water bottle, electrolyte powder, and some healthy snacks. Maybe include ashwagandha pills or an anti-stress herbal combination for anxiety. If you deal with pain, bring whatever helps (meds, patches, cream).

When you arrive at the airport

Tell them you're there and ready for a wheelchair. You could also ask for an "invisible disability" lanyard to help get you through security and boarding faster.

Once past security

Fill up a water bottle or two and buy a sports drink. If you're planning to eat in the airport before your flight, choose one of the kiosks, cafes, or restaurants that specialize in fresh food and healthy choices. Avoid greasy food.

Stay well hydrated on the flight!

Add electrolyte powder to your water, or alternate sipping from a water bottle and a (low-sugar) sports drink.

Plan to rest the day of your arrival, as well as the following day, if possible. Or take several rests/naps. Best to book activities starting the day after that, if you can manage it.

Try to relax and enjoy the experience!

Calm your nervous system and minimize stress to help your body cope with the extra demands on your energy.

Be sure to pace yourself while away.

Sit down for frequent rests. The excitement of travel can give you an adrenaline rush, which could be mistaken for true energy. It's not, and if you overdo it, you could crash before you get home.

Hospital Go-Bag

If you have a complex chronic condition or any other health condition or comorbidity, it's essential to have a go-bag ready in case you have to go to the hospital in a hurry.

Most important items to include:

- Detailed list of prescription meds, over-the-counter meds, and supplements

- List of allergies

- List of current and past health conditions

- List of surgeries and procedures

- List of your doctors and their specialties

- Names and numbers of family members

A card listing priorities about yourself

Most ER employees are unfamiliar with our illnesses and how they affect us. The card listing priorities about you must identify your disabilities. Hospital staff seem to take it more seriously when the word *disability* is used.

Personal essentials:

- Water bottles

- Gatorade or other electrolytes

- Eye mask

- Ear plugs

- Lip balm

- Wet wipes

- Tissues

- Face cleanser

- Face lotion

- Body lotion

- Deodorant

- Nail clippers

- Small scissors

- Extra-long phone charger

- Charging block for your phone cord

- Snacks, protein bars, crackers, protein powder

- Warm socks, slippers

- Underwear

- Pajamas

- A comfy change of clothes

- Comfy, warm cardigan sweater

- Book or e-reader (Kindle)

- Coloring book or puzzle or word search book

- A craft project you're working on

Last-minute list:

Make up a list of last-minute items to add, like your meds and supplements, your cell phone and charger, and anything else you use on a day-to-day basis.

Mobility Aids: Canes, Walkers, Wheelchairs, Scooters

Using a cane, walker, wheelchair, or mobility scooter for the first time, especially in public, can seem like a huge, intimidating step. It can be a real hurdle to get over psychologically to publicly admit that you need some help to get around outside. You also might worry about being judged by others because, unlike those with a missing limb or broken leg, your disability is invisible.

But if using a mobility aid will make the difference between staying home and going to a special event, nearby shops, or a park with family or friends, it's really a no-brainer, isn't it?

If you want to go out, give yourself permission to use whatever it takes to get you there and prevent exhaustion later and PEM the next day.

With the right mobility aid to help you function, your narrow, mostly homebound world will open back up. You'll be able to go on walks, attend outdoor events, and shop in person again. And hopefully, you'll feel fine the next day rather than having the crash you would get from standing in lines and walking long distances.

Canes and Walkers

Cane or walking stick: If you have muscle weakness that affects your legs and arms, as well as orthostatic intolerance that causes you to feel wobbly or dizzy, it's important for your safety to use at least a cane when walking. A fall could change your life for the worse. Also, being able to lean on something while walking saves energy.

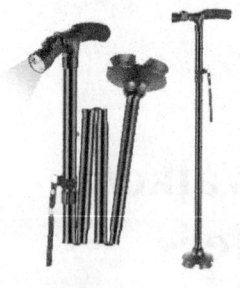

Choose a height-adjustable cane with a firm, wider rubber base and some padding on the handpiece to save your palm. When using it, your arm should be slightly bent at the elbow, not straight. Also, look for one with a loop to slip your hand into to avoid dropping the cane. They come in a variety of bases and colors, and some are foldable.

Cane with 3 legs and a fold-up seat

Handy for when you need to stand in line or walk where there are no benches to rest on.

Forearm crutches

Two-wheel walker: These fold up and are much lighter and less expensive than a four-wheel walker.

Rollator (four-wheel) walker:

Considerations:

When do you plan to use it?

Is it more important to get a lightweight one that you can fold up and easily lift onto the floor of the back seat of your vehicle? (Rather than having to lift it up to the seat or the trunk.)

Or will you mainly be using it for going for walks near your home and to nearby shops? In that case, you'd probably be better off using a sturdier model with a more comfortable seat and a carry basket.

Choosing and using a walker or rollator:

- Make sure it has brakes and the seat is comfortable enough to perch for short (or possibly long) periods.

- Your elbows should be slightly bent when standing and holding the handles.

- When using it, keep your back straight and stand as tall as possible. Be careful not to hunch.

Wheelchairs and Scooters

It's important to choose the right wheelchair or scooter for you, your size, and your needs. You'll need to find one that's:

- A good fit for you physically

- Comfortable for long-term use

- Appropriately sized and maneuverable for where you plan to use it

Important consideration: Many of us have autonomic dysfunction such as orthostatic intolerance or POTS. If you have trouble standing or sitting upright for long, it's important to find a wheelchair or scooter that allows you to elevate your feet and hopefully even lean your torso back if needed. These two options will help avoid blood pooling at your feet and subsequent light-headedness.

Should I buy a wheelchair or a mobility scooter?

Maneuverability: Scooters can be difficult to maneuver in small spaces, whereas wheelchairs are easier to steer and turn.

Ease of transport: You also need to consider how you'll transport it. A small wheelchair may fold up small enough to fit in your trunk. For a scooter, you'll need a platform on the back of your car or a special van with a lift, as they're large and heavy.

Or rent. If you don't need a wheelchair or scooter for daily use but want one for a special event, such as going on vacation, you may want to check into rentals.

Wheelchairs

Manual or power?

Manual (push) wheelchairs are less expensive and usually lighter, but many of us have weak arms and legs, so propelling ourselves forward by turning the wheels can be exhausting. And many of us live alone or would rather not have to ask others to push us whenever we want to go out.

Power wheelchairs (power chairs or electric wheelchairs) are, of course, more expensive, but they offer independence and more convenient mobility while allowing you stay within your energy envelope.

Financial considerations:

Check into the possibility of getting financial help for a power chair from private insurance or your local health authority. Or pay for it on installments. If you have health insurance, consult with your provider to determine whether a wheelchair is covered by your policy and requires a prescription.

Essential Features of a Power Wheelchair for Someone with ME/CFS

When selecting a power wheelchair for yourself or someone else with ME/CFS, it's critical to prioritize comfort, mobility, and ease of use. Consult with an occupational therapist who specializes in mobility devices to help you choose a power wheelchair that meets your specific requirements.

Comfortable seating. Ensure the wheelchair has a well-padded and ergonomic seat with adjustable features such as recline, tilt, and height. Gel or memory foam cushions can help with comfort.

Customizable seating options. Proper seating support (seat width, depth, and height) is vital for comfort and posture.

Adjustable, supportive backrest. Crucial for maintaining proper posture and reducing the risk of back pain. If possible, get a chair with a backrest that can tilt backwards.

Adjustable armrests and footrests. Look for armrests and footrests that can be adjusted to accommodate your height and different body positions and provide optimal support.

Smooth suspension can help absorb shocks and vibrations, providing a smoother ride and reducing fatigue caused by jarring movements.

Easy maneuverability. Choose a power wheelchair with precise and responsive controls for easy turning and maneuvering, even in tight spaces.

Easy transportability. Look for a lightweight and foldable design if the wheelchair needs to be transported frequently.

Safety features. Look for safety features like anti-tip wheels, seatbelts, and a horn.

Long battery life. Opt for a power wheelchair with a long-lasting battery. A removable or swappable battery would be even more convenient.

Maintenance and service. Ensure that the manufacturer or dealer provides reliable maintenance and servicing options to keep the wheelchair in optimal working condition.

Mobility Scooters

It's best to try out mobility scooters before buying one. Sit on a few models and give at least one of them a test drive to see how you get through doors and around corners. Practice backing up and driving on a variety of surfaces, such as a sidewalk, a dirt path, and grass.

Features to Consider When Buying a Mobility Scooter

- Do you fit into it well? Is there enough room for your legs?

- Can you adjust the seat up and down?

- Does the chair rotate from side to side for easy entrance and exit?

- Do the armrests adequately support your arms?

- Do the armrests tilt up out of the way so you can get in and out easily?

- Can you move the steering closer to save your arms?

- How will you transport it? Can it be easily taken apart or folded? Or will you need to purchase a trailer hitch and a scooter lift to pull it behind your vehicle?

Bottom line:

Remember that using a mobility aid when you need it will allow you to get out and widen your world again without suffering afterward and risking your condition getting worse. Taking care of yourself and avoiding post-exertional malaise has to be your number-one priority! And getting out will help your emotional health.

PHYSICAL ACTIVITY

What About Exercise?

In the past, physicians recommended graded exercise therapy, where the intensity and duration of exercise increased slowly and steadily. This approach is now generally considered very risky for people with ME/CFS, as the post-exertional malaise (PEM) that often follows exercise for us can worsen our condition.

According to the Journal of Orthopaedic & Sports Physical Therapy, April 30, 2021,

"The history of ME/CFS with exercise is one of false hope. More than 3 decades of trying exercise in this population can be summed up in one sentence: exercise can be harmful, sometimes life threatening, and should be avoided."

"Graded exercise therapy (GET) should no longer be used to treat patients with myalgic encephalomyelitis ... (ME/CFS), says the National Institute for Health and Care Excellence in long awaited updated guidance. ... "Energy management should consider all types of activity (cognitive, physical, emotional, and social) that help patients learn to use the amount of energy they have, while reducing their risk of post-exertional malaise or worsening their symptoms by exceeding their limits."

The bottom line: Graded exercise therapy is no longer recommended. In fact, it's now considered harmful. **Attempt only mild exercise and proceed with caution.** Pay attention to your body and assess your level of fatigue the day after exercising and two and three days later, since PEM (a crash) can be delayed up to 72 hours.

Some Guidelines for Exercising Safely:

Always exercise with caution.

If you're in the mild (functioning, including outside the home) category and can manage, with frequent rests, a modified version of what your friends and peers can do to exercise, your main goal needs to be to not exacerbate your situation by overdoing it.

Don't give in to peer pressure.

Make it clear to your exercise buddies that you can't manage the full activity and will have to modify the intensity and duration.

And don't feel badly about it or let them pressure you. Nothing is more important than your health, and it's frighteningly easy to make it worse and then have to give up those activities altogether.

Modify the duration and intensity of your activities.

If your friends are hiking up a mountain or hill, go as far as you know you can without paying dearly later. Then sit and rest. Tell them you'll wait there and catch up with them on their way down. Relax and take some photos of your surroundings, or even find a spot to recline and close your eyes. (Take sunglasses and a hat.)

If you want to join your friends cycling, buy or rent an e-bike so you can keep up with them.

Perhaps you can only play three to five holes when golfing or dance for an hour, including rests. That's okay, and smart. It means you're being proactive and in charge of your own health. The most important thing is to not let others pressure you (or pressure yourself) into continuing when you're tired. To avoid getting worse, it's critical to pay attention to your body.

Avoid strenuous activities.

Be sure to avoid overly strenuous or sustained vigorous (aerobic) activities. Those spell overexertion, which could cause permanent harm.

According to the Centers for Disease Control and Prevention (CDC),

"While vigorous aerobic exercise can be beneficial for many chronic illnesses, **patients with ME/CFS do not tolerate such exercise routines**. Standard exercise recommendations for healthy people can be harmful for patients with ME/CFS."

Do only what you can tolerate without payback.

On the other hand, CDC asserts that it's important to maintain physical activities that we are able to tolerate without a flare-up, in order to avoid deconditioning.

"Patients who are tolerating their current level of activity and have learned to 'listen to their bodies' might benefit from carefully increasing exercise to improve their physical fitness and avoid deconditioning."

"However, ME/CFS is unpredictable. PEM symptoms may not start right after exercise, making it important for each treatment plan to be tailored for each case."

You may not be ready yet for exercise.

Many of us struggle with orthostatic intolerance (difficulty staying upright), a condition that needs to be addressed first before attempting any exercise than involves staying upright for more than a few minutes. See the chapter on Orthostatic Intolerance.

According to the CDC, "If exercise plans are not designed and executed carefully, patients may experience setbacks and serious deterioration in function and health. Expectations need to be managed, as exercise cannot be expected to be a cure."

It cannot be overemphasized that "Exercise is not a cure for ME/CFS."

If your condition is at a moderate level, it's critical to stay within your current energy envelope when considering activities and allow your malfunctioning mitochondria to heal.

Your biggest challenge is to be constantly mindful to not overdo it and learn to adjust to less activity than before.

If your body is crying out for rest, don't push through!

Stop and rest!

How to Avoid Deconditioning without Crashing

As mentioned above, if you overexert or push yourself too hard, you risk PEM (post-exertional malaise), which could set you back considerably. The general advice is to do gentle exercises within your energy envelope, increasing very gradually on your good days only. Never push yourself if your body tells you you're tired. You may find that you need to stop for a while and start again later at the beginning level.

Tips for Preventing Deconditioning

To help prevent or reverse deconditioning, consider trying these activities while staying within your own personal limits and energy envelope:

Practice isometric exercises.

These exercises involve contracting your muscles without actually moving your body. Isometrics squeeze your muscles and push your blood back toward your heart. They're simple to do, and you can do them lying in bed or seated. It's a good idea to do these in bed before getting up to prepare your body for sitting and standing.

Stretch your muscles.

- If you're bedbound, even wriggling your toes and fingers, bending your feet at the ankles, rotating your wrists, and slowly moving your arms and legs will help.

- Look up "bed yoga" on YouTube.

- Try chair yoga, yin yoga, seated tai chi, qigong, or any other stretching activities.

- Search YouTube for "Yoga for ME"

- Consider wall Pilates, especially for seniors.

Walk, either unaided or with a cane or walker.

    First, walk around inside your home.

    Then take short walks outside, building up the time and distance very slowly (over months) while paying close attention to how your body responds, both that day and the following days.

    If you experience PEM, take a break and, when ready, restart, but with fewer steps and less frequency.

Lift light weights, but only when feeling at your best.

Use a vibration plate to help relax and tone your muscles, or a seated exercise bike.

Bottom Line:

Exercise mindfully, with caution.

When exercising, always listen to your body and stop any exercise if it exacerbates your symptoms.

Start with very short sessions and gradually increase the duration or intensity only when you feel comfortable.

Pay attention to how you feel the next day and the following days. Cut back or take a break if needed.

Consult with your healthcare provider, physical therapist, or a specialist in ME/CFS to create a personalized exercise plan tailored to your specific needs and limitations.

Gentle Exercises

For the elderly and people with ME/CFS or other chronic conditions, it's essential to approach exercise with caution. Be sure to consult your trusted healthcare professional before starting any new exercise routine.

The following are some gentle, low-impact exercises that you might find manageable and beneficial for staying flexible and increasing or maintaining your muscle strength.

Remember to start slowly and gradually increase intensity and duration only as tolerated.

Deep breathing exercises

Practice deep breathing to help improve oxygenation and reduce stress. Sit or lie down comfortably and take slow, deep breaths, inhaling for a count of four and exhaling for a count of four.

Relaxation techniques

Practice relaxation exercises like mindfulness meditation or progressive muscle relaxation. Start at your toes and work up to your head, tightening and relaxing the muscles of your toes, feet, calves, etc.

Isometric Exercises

Isometric exercises involve contracting muscles without moving your joints. Examples include gently pushing your hands together, squeezing a soft ball, or tightening your buttocks.

Range of motion exercises

To maintain mobility, gently flex your joints – your ankles, knees, elbows, shoulders, and hips. Some examples: shrug your shoulders and rotate them forward a few circles, then backward. Rotate your feet at the ankles. While standing or sitting, raise your right knee, then your left. Rotate your hips gently, like you're using a hoola-hoop. Standing with your feet apart and your hands on hips, slowly rotate your torso forward, around, and up or slightly back. Rotate the other way.

Swimming or water exercises

Water exercises can be less fatiguing, and the buoyancy of water can also reduce the impact on joints and muscles.

Seated Exercises

Perform the following exercises while sitting in a sturdy chair without armrests.

Neck stretches

Gently tilt your head to one side, hold for a few seconds, then repeat on the other side. Or start at one side, go down the front, then up to the other side.

Shoulder stretches

To help relieve aching shoulders, grasp your right elbow with your left hand and push toward your left shoulder. Repeat on the other side. Put your right hand behind your head, then grasp your right elbow and push down gently. Try to see how far down your right hand can go behind your head without straining. Repeat with the other elbow.

Hand and finger exercises

Work on dexterity and strength with simple hand exercises such as these: Touch the corresponding fingers and thumbs of both hands together, like a spider on mirror, and press together and release, several times. Gently rotate your hands at the wrists, both ways. Make fists, then flatten out your hands. Repeat several times.

Arm exercises

Make slow, controlled circles with your arms. Lift your hands in the air, then down to your sides. Arms bent, move your elbows back. Repeat several times.

Ankle exercises

Lift one foot off the ground, rotate your ankle in a circular motion one way, then the other. Switch to the other foot and do the same. Tap your toes on the floor as quickly as you can.

Seated marches

Sit on a sturdy chair with your feet flat on the floor. Lift one knee and then the other, mimicking a marching motion.

Seated leg lifts

Sit with your feet flat on the floor. Lift one leg straight up, hold for a few seconds, and lower it back down. Repeat with the other leg. You may need to hold onto the chair.

Seated rowing

Sit on a chair with your feet flat and pretend to row a boat, pulling your arms backward and squeezing your shoulder blades together.

Arm raises

While standing or sitting, raise your arms up and down a few times. Then, if ready, try holding a lightweight object in each hand (cans of soup or water bottles work) and raise your arms to shoulder height. Lower and repeat.

Seated bicycling

Sit on a chair and mimic pedaling a bicycle. This is a low-impact way to work your leg muscles and improve joint mobility.

Standing Exercises

Calf raises

Stand behind a chair for support and raise up on your toes, then lower your heels back down. This helps strengthen your calf muscles.

Wall push-ups

Stand facing a wall with your palms against it at shoulder height. Slowly lean in and push back out to work your upper body. Repeat several times.

Hip flexor stretch

Stand beside a sturdy chair or counter for balance and lift one knee toward your chest. Hold for a few seconds and switch to the other leg. If this is too difficult, do it while lying on your back.

Standing balance exercises

With one hand lightly on a countertop or sturdy chair for support, lift one foot off the ground and balance on the other for 30 seconds. Switch to the other foot. Gradually, try it with holding on with only two fingers, then one finger, then, if able, with your hand hovering above the support.

Marching in place

Move your arms as well.

Mindful walking

Take short, slow walks, preferably outdoors, focusing on your breath and surroundings. If you need a cane or walker, be sure to use it.

Stationary cycling

If you have access to a stationary bike, use it at a low resistance level and for short durations to improve cardiovascular fitness gradually.

Classes and Practices for Stretching, Flexibility, and Relaxation

Consider checking out YouTube videos or attending in-person classes for gentle yoga, Tai Chi, Pilates, Qigong, or mindful meditation. I suggest starting with YouTube videos at home, to avoid the subliminal pressure of others in the class whose abilities are higher than yours.

Tai Chi

Tai Chi is a gentle, flowing martial art that can enhance balance, coordination, flexibility, and body awareness. For people with ME/CFS who may experience dizziness or unsteadiness, Tai Chi can be a valuable practice to improve physical stability without overexertion. It also emphasizes mindful breathing and relaxation, which makes it an excellent tool in our stress-management toolbox.

Pilates

Pilates can be helpful for people with ME/CFS due to its low-impact nature and focus on core strength, flexibility, and body awareness. Because our two main symptoms are muscle weakness and fatigue, Pilates can help us gradually build strength without overexertion. The controlled movements and emphasis on breath can also promote relaxation and stress reduction. Start on a day you have the energy, with basic, non-strenuous exercises that focus on flexibility, and adapt them to suit your own energy and mobility levels.

Yoga

Yoga can help improve flexibility and reduce stress. Be sure to tart with beginner-level yoga classes or videos that focus on gentle poses and relaxation techniques. Yin Yoga and Restorative Yoga are especially appropriate as they don't require muscular effort.

Yin Yoga

Yin Yoga is beneficial for those with ME/CFS because it involves holding gentle, passive stretches for extended periods, which can improve flexibility and reduce muscle tension without excessive physical strain. The slow-paced nature of Yin Yoga also encourages mindfulness and deep relaxation, which can aid in managing pain and fatigue.

Restorative Yoga

Restorative Yoga is particularly helpful for people with limited energy as it involves passive and supported poses designed to promote relaxation and relieve fatigue. It can improve circulation, reduce pain, and enhance sleep quality, all of which are crucial aspects of managing ME/CFS symptoms.

Qigong

Qigong, like Tai Chi, emphasizes gentle movements, deep breathing, and meditation. It can be especially helpful for people with ME/CFS as it promotes energy flow, reduces stress, and enhances mental clarity. Qigong's low-intensity exercises can be adapted to varying energy levels, making it accessible for those with fluctuating symptoms.

Easy Bed Exercises

Exercise can be challenging for those of us with limited energy and stamina, due to the potential for causing post-exertional malaise (also called a "crash," payback, or relapse).

Here are some gentle bed exercises that may be suitable for the elderly and people with ME/CFS or another condition, especially those who are unable to go out to yoga classes, for walks, or even walk a lot around the home.

Remember to approach all exercise with caution and adaptability, keeping in mind your limitations and any movements that could exacerbate your back, neck, or any other condition you have.

Deep breathing

Lie on your back, close your eyes, and take slow, deep breaths. Focus on inhaling for a count of four, holding for a count of four, and exhaling for a count of four. Deep breathing can help relax your body and reduce stress.

Isometric contractions

While lying down, gently press your palms together, creating resistance without moving your hands. Hold for a few seconds, then relax. Repeat with other muscle groups, like your thighs, buttocks, or biceps.

Gentle neck stretches

While lying on your back, gently tilt your head to the left, holding for a few seconds, then to the right. Repeat this motion for a few minutes to relieve neck tension. You can also try making a semicircle with your chin: right side, dip down to chest, up to left side, hold, then down and back.

Heel slides

Lie on your back with your legs straight. Bend one knee, sliding your heel along the bed towards your buttocks. Slowly return your leg to its original position and repeat on the other side. This exercise helps with hip flexibility.

Ankle pumps and rotations

Lie on your back and move your feet up and down at the ankles, as if you're pressing the gas pedal in a car. Then rotate each foot at the ankle. These movements will help prevent stiffness and improve your circulation.

Knee raises

While lying on your back, bend one knee and bring it toward your chest. Hold for a few seconds, then switch legs. If you have back problems, it's safest to start with both knees bent. Once one is at your chest, lower the other knee to straight leg position. Return it to bent knee before changing sides. Also, if you have back problems, try aiming the raised knee toward the opposite shoulder. This exercise can help with flexibility and blood flow.

Stretches for thighs and hips

On your back, start with your legs straight down, then gradually move them as far out to each side as you can. Rest there for a minute or so, then back to the center, then knees up. Knees down and repeat.

Arm angels and circles

Lie on your back with your arms out to the sides. Move them up and down on the bed, like you're making a snow angel. Then, if you can, lift your arms straight up toward the ceiling and make small circles in the air, gradually increasing the size of the circles. Stop if tired. These exercises can help with arm strength and upper body mobility.

Pelvic tilts

Lie on your back with your knees bent. Gently tilt your pelvis up towards the ceiling, then back down. This exercise can help alleviate lower back pain. Be sure to keep your knees bent.

Bicycling

If able, try bicycling (pedaling) in the air. Stop if it's too much or hurts your back.

Deep relaxation

Practice progressive muscle relaxation by tensing and then relaxing each muscle group in your body, starting from your toes and working your way up to your head.

Bottom line:

Remember that the key to managing ME/CFS is pacing and not pushing yourself too hard. Start with just a few minutes of these exercises and gradually increase the duration or intensity if your body allows. Listen to your body and rest when needed.

Check in with yourself the next day. Did the exercises make you feel better and help you sleep? Or did you overdo it? If so, dial back on the frequency, intensity, and duration.

ADVICE FOR FAMILY AND FRIENDS

How to be Supportive

Listen. Accept. Be Careful about Giving Advice.

Does someone in your family or circle of friends have ME/CFS (chronic fatigue syndrome), long COVID, Lyme disease, fibromyalgia, MS, lupus, or another condition that causes extreme fatigue, muscle weakness, and difficulty concentrating and communicating? Or are they simply getting on in age and don't have the energy they used to?

Here are some tips for being empathetic and understanding while keeping your friendship or relationship intact.

DOs:

- Realize that just carrying on a conversation can be really exhausting, so don't be insulted if they don't return your call, text, or email for a while or if they end a phone conversation or in-person visit sooner than you expected.

- Before calling, text them to ask, "Are you up for a phone call?" or "When would be a good time for a chat on the phone?"

- Know that they'll sometimes or often need to cancel plans when they're just too tired to go out. Be understanding when this happens.

- Invite them to events or outings anyway, as that will make them feel better even if they have to decline. Try to word your invitation in a way that tells them they're welcome to come but that you understand and won't be offended if they're ultimately not feeling well enough to come.

239

DON'Ts:

- Don't tell them you feel sorry for them. Or indicate it in any way. Your pity will only make them feel worse. Acceptance, empathy, and compassion are much better than overt sympathy.

- Don't assume they're "just depressed." That theory was refuted decades ago.

- Don't say, "You're too young to be tired," or "You're too young to need a wheelchair." (Or cane or walker.) That feels like you're implying they're somehow to blame for their condition.

- Don't say, "You look fine." That implies you think they're lying or are a hypochondriac. People with ME/CFS tend to look fine from the outside. The exhaustion, weakness, and pain are all inside.

- Avoid saying, "Think positive." This sounds dismissive, like you'd rather not hear about their condition, or you think they're not doing enough or should ignore their limitations.

- Don't hint that maybe it's all in their head and they just need counselling.

- Don't tell them they just need to get more exercise. This is well-meaning but harmful advice that could cause long-term or permanent damage. See the section on exercise.

- If they complain about being too tired or weak to do a task or activity, don't ever tell them to just do it and push through their fatigue. This is the worst possible advice!

- Don't hold them to the same housekeeping and cooking standards they had before or that you and others have. They need to conserve their energy, and their health is much more important than a spotless home and gourmet meals.

- Don't say, "But you were able to do that yesterday," or "I saw you working earlier, so surely you can do this now." It's extremely likely that they're now in recovery mode from working too hard or doing too much yesterday or earlier. Their earlier exertion could even have caused PEM (post-exertional malaise) or a crash.

240

- Don't say, "I saw you walking the other day, so why do you need a [cane/walker/wheelchair] today? People with ME have good days and bad days. Others rarely see them on their worst days because they don't go out and could even be bedbound for days.

- It's nice of you to say, "Let me know if you need anything." But it would be so much better and more helpful, especially if they're housebound or bedbound, if you said, "What can I do for you right now?" Or, "Can I pick you up something from the grocery store?"

- Better yet, do something specific for the person without them having to ask. Pick up their mail, tidy their kitchen, load or unload their dishwasher, water their plants, or drop off dinner.

- Don't say, "Have you tried (therapy/food/exercise)? (Unless you're an expert on it.) This can be really frustrating, as they likely know so much more about their condition than you do, including all the advice that doesn't help.

Basically, it's best to steer away from giving advice at all, as many of the habits that help healthy people, such as getting more exercise or going out more and socializing, don't work for people with a chronic fatigue condition.

If you're close to them, you could gently ask if they're getting fresh air, finding ways to relax and/or get out in nature, doing some stretches or easy yoga, going for short walks if able, eating nutritious food, taking a multivitamin, avoiding too much sugar, and staying hydrated. Those general good habits, while no means a cure, will help them feel better.

If you stay at their home as a guest:

Bring food and snacks, pitch in and help, allow them to nap and rest, and don't expect them to entertain you.

Also, don't have the TV or music on loud or all the time, and don't expect long conversations with them. As much as they'd like to chat and catch up, listening to details and trying to formulate appropriate responses can be exhausting.

241

ADDITIONAL INFORMATION ON
ME/CFS & OTHER CONDITIONS

Myalgic Encephalomyelitis/Chronic Fatigue Syndrome

ME/CFS: Levels of Severity

How Severe Can ME/CFS Get?

The definitions below, compiled from NICE.org and the CDC, provide a guide to the level of impact of symptoms on everyday functioning.

Mild ME/CFS

People with mild ME/CFS care for themselves and do some light domestic tasks (sometimes needing support) but may have difficulties with mobility. Most are still working or in education, but to do this, they've probably stopped all leisure and social pursuits. They often have reduced hours, take days off, and use the weekend to cope with the rest of the week.

Moderate ME/CFS

People with moderate ME/CFS have reduced mobility and are restricted in all activities of daily living, although they may have peaks and troughs in their level of symptoms and ability to do activities. They've usually stopped work or education, and they need rest periods, often resting in the afternoon for 1 or 2 hours. Their sleep at night is generally poor quality and disturbed.

Severe ME/CFS

People with severe ME/CFS are unable to do any activity for themselves or can carry out only minimal daily tasks (such as face washing or cleaning teeth). They have severe cognitive difficulties and may depend on a wheelchair for mobility. They're often unable to leave the house or have a severe and prolonged after-effect if they do so. They may also spend most of their time in bed and are often extremely sensitive to light and sound.

Very severe ME/CFS

People with very severe ME/CFS are in bed all day and dependent on care. They need help with personal hygiene and eating, and they're very sensitive to sensory stimuli. Some people may not be able to swallow and may need to be tube-fed.

Resources used for this section on levels of severity:

NICE – National Institute for Health and Care Excellence, UK:

https://www.nice.org.uk/guidance/ng206/chapter/recommendations#box-1-severity-of-mecfs

Levels of Severity in People with ME/CFS:

CDC: Treatment of ME/CFS | Myalgic Encephalomyelitis/Chronic Fatigue Syndrome (ME/CFS) | CDC

Causes of ME/CFS

What are some of the causes of ME/CFS?

According to the Mayo Clinic, the cause of chronic fatigue syndrome is still unknown. A combination of factors may be involved, including:

- **Infections:** Some people develop chronic fatigue syndrome symptoms after a viral or bacterial infection.

- **Physical or emotional trauma:** An injury, surgery, or significant emotional stress can deplete the body's resources and lead to ME/CFS.

- **Problems with energy usage:** Many people with chronic fatigue syndrome have problems converting the body's fuel (from oxygen, water, food, and beverages) into useable energy. (See the chapter "Malfunctioning Mitochondria.")

- **Genetics:** Chronic fatigue syndrome appears to run in some families, so some people may be born with a higher likelihood of developing the disorder.

Also, according to other sites, another cause might be:

- **Exposure to toxic chemicals and fumes:** Trying to function in a chemically toxic environment can shock and deplete the system.

Malfunctioning Mitochondria

ME/CFS is a very complex condition with a wide range of potential contributing factors, including immune system dysfunction, neuroinflammation, hormonal imbalances, mitochondrial dysfunction, and more.

Researchers are actively investigating these various factors to better understand the condition and develop effective treatments.

One of the leading theories about the underlying causes of fatigue, physical weakness, brain fog, and other symptoms of ME/CFS suggests that our limited energy is likely due to damaged mitochondria.

Why can't my body produce more energy?

As Dr. Sarah Myhill says in Diagnosis and Treatment of Chronic Fatigue and Myalgic Encephalitis,

"It's Mitochondria, Not Hypochondria."

According to Dr. Myhill (and others), the debilitating fatigue, muscle weakness, cognitive difficulties, and lack of stamina in people with CFS/ME are all caused by mitochondrial dysfunction.

As she says,

"Mitochondria are the 'engines' of our bodies. These 'organelles' (microstructures within cells) are present in the vast majority of cells and are responsible for generating energy."

Myhill asserts that the central cause of CFS/ME is mitochondrial failure.

246

From my research for this book, it appears that the initial mitochondrial failure is most likely caused by a severe shock to the system, brought on by a traumatic event, a virus, extended stress, exposure to toxic chemicals, or extreme physical or mental overexertion.

How can we help our mitochondria strengthen and heal?

We can nurture our bodies by:

- resting frequently

- avoiding stress

- staying hydrated

- eating nourishing food

- taking a quality multivitamin,

- avoiding sugar, alcohol, and chemicals

- taking certain supplements known for helping mitochondria.

Myhill's "mitochondrial package of supplements":

She recommends Co-Q10, niacinamide (not niacin, which causes flushing), L-carnitine, D-ribose, magnesium, glutathione, and vitamin B12.

For additional information on possibly helpful supplements, see the chapter, "Supplements."

Orthostatic Intolerance

Do you find heat, showering, and/or standing exhausting?

Many people with ME/CFS have to deal with **orthostatic intolerance, difficulty staying upright**. For some, their OI is so severe that they can hardly stand and are mostly or entirely bedbound. Others might need to use a cane, walker, or wheelchair to move around. Standing seems to be worse than walking, and even sitting upright for extended periods of time can be exhausting, so it's often better to recline or lie down.

According to an educational PDF created by the Bateman Horne Center in October 2022, Orthostatic-Intolerance-Education-Handout-10_2022-.pdf (batemanhornecenter.org)

"Orthostatic intolerance (OI) refers to the development of symptoms when standing that are relieved by lying down."

Blood pools in the feet and hands, with decreased blood return to the heart and lungs, resulting in reduced cardiac output to the brain and body. Some people experience dizziness or heart palpitations.

Orthostatic Intolerance is common in ME/CFS and long COVID, and it can also occur in those with fibromyalgia.

The information below is paraphrased from material in the excellent handout by the Bateman Horne Center.

Some factors and activities that may cause or worsen OI:

- Being upright (in one spot) for longer than is comfortable or tolerable:
  - Standing in line

- Standing while talking to someone
  - Cooking or washing dishes
  - Sitting upright for too long
- Heat:
  - Hot weather
  - A hot, crowded room
  - A hot bath or shower
- Exercise or any exertion
- Stress
- Eating a large meal and/or hard-to-digest food

Common Symptoms of Orthostatic Intolerance Include:

After standing up or while standing or sitting upright for too long:

Sudden fatigue, light-headedness or fainting, palpitations or heart pounding, headaches, mental confusion, chest discomfort, cold hands and feet, and more.

Treatment of OI

The Bateman Horne Center suggests:

Increase daily intake of sodium and water:

- Drink a minimum of 2 liters of water or other fluids.

- Consume a minimum of 2 glasses within the first hour of rising in the morning, 2 glasses before lunch, 1 glass with lunch, 2 glasses in the afternoon, and 1 glass with dinner,

  - AND

- Half of the fluid intake should have added electrolytes.

  Note: Be sure to consult with your medical provider(s) before increasing sodium/fluid intake in the event this is contraindicated for your condition(s).

Electrolyte drinks include Pedialyte, Liquid IV, Nuun, Drip Drop, LMNT, GatorLyte, Hydromate, and other Oral Rehydration Solutions.

Bateman Horne also recommends:

- Wear compression clothing. Compression stockings will help avoid blood pooling in your feet and calves.

- Eat small but frequent meals

- Avoid alcohol and caffeine

- Avoid exercise within an hour after a meal

- Exercise is often better tolerated when lying down or seated.

If you know you'll have to stand for a while or you're about to have a shower or go for a walk, they suggest rapidly drinking two glasses (500 mL) of cold water first.

(Permission granted from the Bateman Horne Center)

POTS

What is postural orthostatic tachycardia syndrome (POTS)?

Postural orthostatic tachycardia syndrome (POTS) is a form of **dysautonomia**—a disorder of the autonomic nervous system. It's a type of orthostatic intolerance that, when you stand up, causes your heart to beat faster than normal and your blood to pool in your lower extremities. Often, your blood pressure drops, and you may experience symptoms such as dizziness, "wobbliness," fainting, and exhaustion.

Postural: related to the position of your body

Orthostatic: related to standing upright

Tachycardia: increased heart rate (over 100 beats per minute)

Syndrome: a group of symptoms that happen together

Is POTS common, and who does it affect?

POTS is quite common. It affects about 1 to 3 million people in the United States. Most people with POTS are women aged 15 to 50 years, but men can also have POTS.

You're at a higher risk of developing POTS after experiencing:

A serious infection, a viral illness such as mononucleosis, physical trauma such as a head injury, pregnancy, or surgery.

If you have POTS, or think you may have, avoid these situations:

- Standing up suddenly.
- Spending time under the hot sun or taking a hot bath or shower, especially on a hot day.

251

- Standing for a long time, such as waiting in line or extended shopping.

- Participating in strenuous exercise.

What are the symptoms of POTS?

According to the Cleveland Clinic, the symptoms of POTS include:

- Dizziness or light-headedness, especially when standing up, during prolonged standing in one position, or on long walks

- Fainting or near fainting

- Forgetfulness and trouble focusing (brain fog)

- Heart palpitations or racing heart rate

- Exhaustion/fatigue

- Feeling nervous or anxious

- Shakiness and excessive sweating

- Chest pain and/or shortness of breath (dyspnea)

- Feeling sick, nausea or vomiting

- Headache

POTS symptoms typically get worse:

In warm environments, such as a hot bath or shower, a hot room or on a hot day

In situations involving a lot of standing, such as waiting for a bus or when shopping

If fluid and salt intake have not been adequate, such as after skipping a meal

How do I prevent light-headedness, "staggering," or dizziness when I stand up?

When you're getting up from bed, sit on the edge of your bed for several minutes to allow your body to adjust to being semi-upright. Once you're standing, pause and wait before walking to allow your blood pressure to adjust again. Then walk slowly. If you feel lightheaded, stop and wait for a few minutes. You may need to sit again and start all over, moving slowly.

Medical compression stockings and/or tight yoga pants can also help push blood up from your legs to reduce POTS symptoms. It's best to put on the compression stockings or tights before getting up.

What is the treatment for POTS?

According to the Cleveland Clinic, the main forms of treatment include:

Try to be active, if possible.

For the best results, the Cleveland Clinic recommends reclined or seated aerobic exercise, such as swimming, rowing, and recumbent bicycling. They also suggest that you begin a modest walking program, practice simple yoga with an emphasis on breathing, and practice isometric exercises.

Do some isometric exercises regularly.

While lying or seated, contract your muscles, such as your buttocks, and release them. Squeezing your muscles will help push your blood back toward your heart. It's a good idea to do these in bed before getting up, to prepare your body for sitting and standing.

Manage your diet and nutrition.

Managing diet and nutrition is another important aspect of controlling POTS symptoms.

The Cleveland Clinic's general guidelines for dietary changes include:

- Increase sodium in your diet to 10,000 mg per day.

- Drink 2 to 2.5 liters per day of fluids. Water is the best choice.

- Eat smaller, more frequent meals instead of a few large meals.

- Choose foods with high fiber and complex carbohydrates rather than refined foods.

- Eat a nutritionally balanced diet.

- Choose beneficial salty snacks such as broth, pickles, olives, sardines, anchovies, and nuts, rather than relying on chips and crackers.

- Avoid alcohol, which can worsen symptoms because it dehydrates your body.

Try to maintain a consistent body temperature.

Temperature extremes, especially heat, can make the symptoms of POTS worse. See "Surviving Hot Summer Weather" in this book for tips on staying cooler during a heat wave.

When showering, it's best to use warm or lukewarm water, as either hot or cold can trigger POTS symptoms.

Avoid prolonged standing.

In the kitchen, use a stool with a footrest. When showering, use a shower chair, stool, or bench.

If you must stand unaided for a long time, try flexing and squeezing your feet and muscles or shifting your weight from one foot to the other. Or try crossing your legs, rocking up and down on your toes, clenching your buttocks and tummy muscles, or clenching your fists.

Work toward better sleep, including raising the head of your bed.

Fibromyalgia

What is fibromyalgia?

Fibromyalgia is a condition that causes pain all over the body, sleep problems, fatigue, memory issues, and often emotional and mental distress. People with fibromyalgia may be more sensitive to pain than people without fibromyalgia.

What causes fibromyalgia?

The cause of fibromyalgia is not known. However, according to the Mayo Clinic, "Symptoms often begin after an event, such as physical trauma, surgery, infection or significant psychological stress. In other cases, symptoms gradually accumulate over time with no single triggering event."

Who does it affect?

Fibromyalgia affects about 2% of the adult population. As in the case of ME/CFS, women are more likely to develop fibromyalgia than are men.

What are the main symptoms of fibromyalgia?

According to the CDC, the most common symptoms of fibromyalgia are:

- Pain and stiffness all over the body
- Fatigue
- Anxiety
- Sleep problems
- Problems with thinking, memory, and concentration

- Depression

- Headaches, including migraines

Other symptoms may include:

- Digestive problems, such as abdominal pain, bloating, constipation, and even IBS

- Tingling or numbness in hands and feet

- Pain in the face or jaw

Can fibromyalgia be treated?

The Mayo Clinic says: "While there is no cure for fibromyalgia, a variety of medications can help control symptoms. Exercise, relaxation and stress-reduction measures also may help."

Resources:

CDC: Fibromyalgia | Arthritis | CDC

Mayo Clinic: Fibromyalgia - Symptoms & causes - Mayo Clinic

Other Possible Conditions or Comorbidities

My personal experience and knowledge base centers around ME/CFS. However, if you have unexplained or undiagnosed chronic fatigue, muscle weakness, brain fog, mobility issues, and/or pain, you might be dealing with one or more of these conditions:

- post-COVID-19 syndrome
- fibromyalgia
- thyroid dysfunction
- adrenal dysfunction
- mast cell activation syndrome (MCAS)
- postural orthostatic tachycardia syndrome (POTS)
- Lyme disease
- Epstein-Barr virus (EBV)
- Ehlers-Danlos syndrome (EDS)
- lupus
- multiple sclerosis (MS)
- attention deficit hyperactivity disorder (ADHD)
- low iron, or other deficiencies of critical nutrients

If you have an undiagnosed condition, be sure to seek qualified professional medical advice and get tested for any of these or other possibilities, so you can receive the specialized help you need.

Other Helpful Techniques to Investigate

Many promising techniques and practices for regaining energy are being studied and used that are outside the scope of this book. Some of those include:

- Brain retraining (neural retraining)

- Body-mind therapy

- Neuroplasticity

- Vagus nerve stimulation or massages

- Isometric exercises

- Manifestation meditations

- Reflexology

- Acupuncture

- Gut health (microbiome)

- Keto diet

A few meds to ask your doctor about that have shown to be useful or promising in providing more energy:

- IV therapy

- Vitamin B12 injections

- Low-dose naltrexone (LDN)

Abbreviations

ADHD – attention deficit hyperactivity disorder

AT – aerobic threshold

CDC – Centers for Disease Control

CFS – chronic fatigue syndrome

CFIDS – chronic fatigue immune deficiency syndrome, an alternative name for ME/CFS

EBV – Epstein-Barr virus

EDS – Ehlers-Danlos syndrome

FM or fibro – fibromyalgia

HR – heart rate

HRV – heart rate variability

LDA – low dose abilify (aripiprazole)

LDN – low dose naltrexone

MCAS – mast cell activation syndrome

ME – myalgic encephalomyelitis

MS – multiple sclerosis

NIH – National Institutes for Health

OI – orthostatic intolerance

PEM – post-exertional malaise (PEM)

PENE - post-exertional neuroimmune exhaustion

PESE – post-exertional symptom exacerbation

POTS – postural orthostatic tachycardia syndrome

RHR – resting heart rate

SEID – Systemic Exertion Intolerance Disease/Disorder, an alternative name for ME/CFS

Did you find this book useful?

I would really appreciate it if you could please leave a review.

If you have found the information and tips in this book useful and think others with limited energy would benefit from it too, please leave a brief review of it wherever you purchased it and/or on Goodreads. That will help the book be visible to anyone searching this topic.

If you have any suggestions for improvement, please contact me, the author, at info@jodierenner.ca.

Thank you very much.

Jodie Renner, M.A.

Works Cited

BOOKS:

Hirsch, Evan H., MD, ABOIM, *Fix Your Fatigue*, 2017.

Myhill, Dr. Sarah, Diagnosis and Treatment of Chronic Fatigue Syndrome and Myalgic Encephalitis, Chelsea Green Publishing, 2017, Vermont, USA.

Teitelbaum, Jacob, M.D. *The Fatigue and Fibromyalgia Solution,* 2013, Avery (Penguin), New York.

WEBSITES:

Bateman Horne Center, https://batemanhornecenter.org/

"The Bateman Horne Center (BHC) is a non-profit, interdisciplinary Center of Excellence where clinical care, research, and education meet to collectively advance the diagnosis and treatment of myalgic encephalomyelitis/chronic fatigue syndrome (ME/CFS), fibromyalgia (FM), post-viral syndromes, and related comorbidities."

- Permission granted by the Bateman Horne Center to quote and paraphrase their excellent information.

Centers for Disease Control and Prevention (CDC): https://www.cdc.gov/me-cfs/index.html

Treatment of ME/CFS | Myalgic Encephalomyelitis/Chronic Fatigue Syndrome (ME/CFS) | CDC

https://www.cdc.gov/me-cfs/healthcare-providers/clinical-care-patients-mecfs/treating-most-disruptive-symptoms.html)

Chronic Illness Inclusion, https://chronicillnessinclusion.org.uk

Cleveland Clinic: https://my.clevelandclinic.org/health/diseases/16560-postural-orthostatic-tachycardia-syndrome-pots

Complex Chronic Diseases Program, BC Women's Hospital, Vancouver, BC, http://www.bcwomens.ca/

Everydayhealth.com. https://www.everydayhealth.com/

"Everyday Health's passionate, award-winning editorial team is committed to supporting you in your journey to live a healthy life each and every day. By adhering to the highest standards for accuracy, objectivity, and balance, we create trustworthy content based on up-to-date, evidence-based health and medical information and real world patient and clinician experience to help inform you how to take control of your health."

Healthline.com

Health Rising, https://www.healthrising.org/. Finding Answers for ME/CFS and FM

Hunter-Hopkins Center, Charlotte, North Carolina.

Dr. Charles Lapp, founder and medical director of the Center, began treating ME/CFS and FM patients in 1985. The clinic specializes in ME/CFS and FM.

Johns Hopkins Medicine, Postural Orthostatic Tachycardia Syndrome (POTS) | Johns Hopkins Medicine

Livescience.com

Mayo Clinic: https://www.mayoclinic.org/diseases-conditions/chronic-fatigue-syndrome/

ME/CFS & Fibromyalgia Self-Help, http://www.cfsselfhelp.org/

"The ME/CFS and Fibromyalgia Self-Help Program is a non-profit organization offering a suite of low-cost and free online self-help courses, plus other resources for people affected by ME/CFS and fibromyalgia. Founded in 1998, it has conducted hundreds of self-help groups teaching thousands of people how to manage their illness."

NICE – National Institute for Health and Care Excellence, UK: https://www.nice.org.uk/

Painscale.com. https://www.painscale.com/article/supplement-options-for-myalgic-encephalomyelitis-chronic-fatigue-syndrome-me-cfs

Workwell Foundation – https://workwellfoundation.org/

> "Workwell's mission is to focus on research concerning the functional aspects of myalgic encephalomyelitis/chronic fatigue syndrome (ME/CFS), long COVID, and other fatigue-related illnesses to facilitate an understanding of the biological basis for fatigue and post-exertional malaise (PEM).

> "Workwell offers unique testing services for individuals with disabling fatigue who are unable to work. In addition, we provide innovative resources to educate patients and providers."

World ME Alliance, information about ME: worldmealliance.org/what-is-me. The World ME Alliance is made up of national ME organisations from across the world. Find your nearest organisation at: worldmealliance.org/our-members.

ONLINE ARTICLES:

Campbell, Bruce. "Nutrition and Chemical Sensitivity." *ME/CFS & FIBROMYALGIA SELF-HELP,* http://www.cfsselfhelp.org/library/nutrition-and-chemical-sensitivity

Campbell, Bruce, "Dr Lapp's Recommendations on Supplements." Updated March 2, 2021, *ME/CFS & Fibromyalgia Self-Help,* http://www.cfsselfhelp.org/library/dr-lapp%27s-recommedations-supplements

Dellwo, Adrienne. "What to Eat When You Have Chronic Fatigue Syndrome." Updated on July 29, 2021, CFS & Fibromyalgia – Living With, https://www.verywellhealth.com/chronic-fatigue-syndrome-fibromyalgia-diet-715718, 2021

Goodson, Amy, MS, RD, CSSD, LD. "The 19 Best Foods to Improve Digestion." Updated on February 14, 2023, Healthline.com. https://www.healthline.com/nutrition/best-foods-for-digestion

Gora, Anna. "Probiotics vs Digestive Enzymes – What's the Difference?" *livescience.com* https://www.livescience.com/probiotics-vs-digestive-enzymes

Hill, Ansley RD, LD. "16 Superfoods That Are Worthy of the Title," Healthline.com, https://www.healthline.com/nutrition/true-superfoods

Jones, Heather "Best and Worst Foods for Gut Health," VeryWellHealth, June 28, 2023. https://www.verywellhealth.com/gut-health-foods-7498022

Torjesen, Ingrid. "ME/CFS: Exercise goals should be set by patients and not driven by treatment plan," Oct. 2021, NICE, https://doi.org/10.1136/bmj.n2643

"Supplement Options for Myalgic Encephalomyelitis/Chronic Fatigue Syndrome (ME/CFS)" (No author provided.)

"Humility and Acceptance: Working Within Our Limits with Long COVID and Myalgic Encephalomyelitis/Chronic Fatigue Syndrome" (April 30, 2021, *Journal of Orthopaedic & Sports Physical Therapy*, https://www.jospt.org/doi/10.2519/jospt.2021.0106)

"Postural Orthostatic Tachycardia Syndrome (POTS)," Cleveland Clinic, https://my.clevelandclinic.org/health/diseases/16560-postural-orthostatic-tachycardia-syndrome-pots

"Postural Tachycardia Syndrome (PoTS)," https://www.nhs.uk/conditions/postural-tachycardia-syndrome/

Acknowledgments

I'd like to thank my smart, generous beta readers for their astute suggestions, all of which helped improve the content and presentation of this book: Laurie Shewchuk, Shirley Maritsch-Tucker, Cherie Hanson, Mary Sklarowa, Nicole Rogers, Summer Romney, and Carrie Warren. Thanks so much for your helpful feedback!

Special thanks to my siblings and to my two sons for their ongoing support and encouragement.

About the Author

Jodie Renner—a former teacher, librarian, book editor, and blogger with a master's degree—is the author of three award-winning craft-of-writing books, *Writing a Killer Thriller, Fire up Your Fiction,* and *Captivate Your Readers*, and two e-resources for writers, and the organizer and editor of two anthologies.

You can visit Jodie's Amazon "About the Author" page at

https://www.amazon.com/stores/Jodie-Renner/author/B008H80AIE

her website at www.jodierenner.ca,

and her blog for writers at

Resources for Writers (jodierennerediting.blogspot.com).

Jodie has been battling chronic fatigue syndrome for over fifty years. Her condition was mainly mild until March 2022, when she pushed herself way too hard on a vacation and her condition worsened to the moderate level. By pacing, guarding her energy, and taking care of her body, Jodie is slowly working back to her previous baseline of mild and functioning, both in and out of the home.

After two and a half years on a waiting list, Jodie was finally formally diagnosed with ME/CFS in October 2021, followed by a year of online classes by the Complex Chronic Diseases Program in Vancouver, BC, Canada.

While enrolled in the program and advancing her knowledge of myalgic encephalomyelitis, Jodie also did a lot of her own research into the condition, reading books and numerous articles from respected sites. Her classes, research, and contact with many, many other people with ME inspired her to share tried-and-true tips to successfully manage this condition and improve our quality of life.

Jodie Renner lives in Kelowna, BC, Canada. Prior to her setback in March 2022, she enjoyed weekly dancing, walks in nature, lunches and dinners with friends, home renos, and photography.

INDEX

270